WHEN
NATURAL
DISASTER
STRIKES

D0869450

WHEN NATURAL DISASTER STRIKES

LESSONS FROM HURRICANE ANDREW

By Rick Eyerdam

Foreword by Jack D. Gordon
President, Hospice Foundation of America

Hospice Foundation of America
Health Council of South Florida

The publisher gratefully acknowledges the *Miami Herald* for granting permission to reproduce the photographs that appear on the cover and throughout the book.

Copies of this book may be ordered by calling the Hospice Foundation of America at (800) 854-3402, or by writing to the following address:

Hospice Foundation of America
Suite 401
777 17th Street
Miami Beach, FL 33139

Book design and cover by New Age Graphics, Bethesda, MD
Typesetting by Edington-Rand, Inc., Riverdale, MD

Publisher's Cataloging in Publication Data

Eyerdam, Rick.
   When natural disaster strikes : lessons from Hurricane Andrew /
by Rick Eyerdam ; foreword by Jack D. Gordon.
   p. cm.
   ISBN 0-929765-36-2

3 1969 00788 0296

1. Emergency management—United States. 2. Emergency medical services—United States—Management. 3. Disaster relief—United States—Management. 4. Hurricane Andrew, 1992.   I. Title.

HV551.3.E94 1994   363.3'48'0973
                                QBI94-2180

TABLE OF CONTENTS

FOREWORD

The idea of sponsoring a study of the response of the health care system during Hurricane Andrew occurred to me when my wife and I traveled to Florida City in the days just after the storm. At that time I was still a Florida state senator, although my tenure would expire within a few months. Our first stop was at an improvised health clinic set up by some emergency health workers from Orlando, who, like many others, just came to Miami on their own to help.

When I saw how complete was the devastation and how inadequate the response, I felt compelled to interject myself to help those affected. For a few chaotic days I moved about, directing troops and other relief workers who were desperate for instruction on where to go and what to do. In truth, I did little more than ratify their efforts as a surrogate authority figure, helping them set priorities while they awaited the arrival of the top links in their chain of command.

I wondered, if things were this worrisome in one location, how difficult could they be in other areas? As we watched the relief effort unwind over the next few weeks, the reports from the traditional media sources were mostly positive and cheering, despite the evidence gathered by those of us who witnessed the process firsthand. The need to be upbeat in the wake of a disaster such as Andrew is a sufficient excuse to account for the one-dimensional reporting of the problems the planners and deliverers of health care were enduring.

It was evident to those of us inside the system that despite the fact that the health care community and public health system in South Florida are populated with intelligent, dedicated individuals who had made a serious effort at planning, the plans did not always achieve their desired purpose. And some things that happened quite by accident proved to be a tremendous success.

We felt that once some semblance of calm had returned, we ought to find some way to make sure that the health care community in South Florida and beyond could look in an unbiased mirror and learn from our successes and failures. We thought that by examining the decision-making process in the midst of the crisis, we would get a view of events that would not be reported in academic inquiries.

To this end the Hospice Foundation of America contracted with the Health Council of South Florida to provide a study of the lessons of Andrew. After consultation, it was agreed that the story would be better told anecdotally. We agreed to fund the Health Council to hire an investigative reporter with substantial experience in health care reporting and let the chips fall where they might.

The result is this book, *When Natural Disaster Strikes: Lessons from Hurricane Andrew.* We have found it to be what we hoped it would be—informative, instructional, and interesting. We hope you agree. We also hope that those who live in areas subject to major natural devastation will find some issues of relevance for their communities.

Jack D. Gordon
President
Hospice Foundation of America

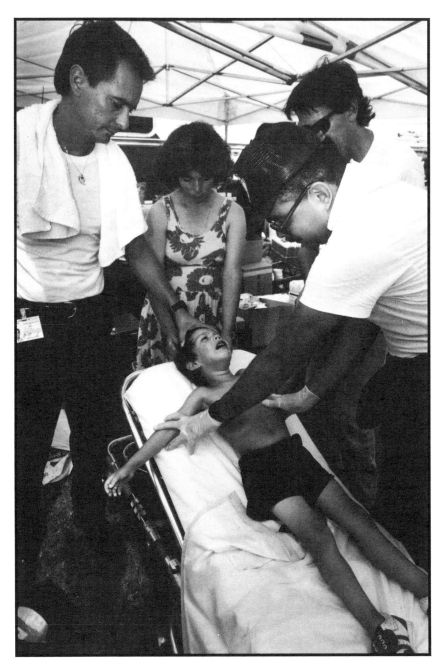

When the eye of the hurricane has passed and its winds have died down, the misery it has left must be handled amidst the devastation and in often primitive conditions. In a clinic set up in a tent, rather than in a traditional hospital emergency room, a young patient is treated for persistent dizziness resulting from a blow to his head from a falling roof.

FROM CLOUD TO CRISIS

In midafternoon on Thursday, August 13, 1992, a fluffy cloud looked down upon the desolate slums of Khartoum, Sudan, offering a fleeting moment of blessed shade. Once out over the vast African veldt, the cloud took a deep breath and latched onto the wind the natives call *Haboob,* which forms a powerful current propelling storm clouds ever westward across Africa's midsection toward the Atlantic. The atmospheric pressure within the cloud dropped slowly as the convection and winds slowly grew, sending a roiling column of warm air and water molecules soaring up near the stratosphere, then plunging back down again.

By the following day, the cloud from Khartoum had become a storm pelting western Senegal with winds and rain. Inspired by the rotation of the planet Earth beneath it, the storm slowly began to spin as it slid over the warm waters off the West African coast. It was mid-August, already the middle of the hurricane season, and not one tropical disturbance had achieved the properties—sustained winds of 39 miles an hour, low pressure, and a definite rotation—to earn a proper name.

On the satellite maps of the National Hurricane Center, 4,000 miles to the west in Coral Gables, Florida, sometime during the day on August 16, the storm that would become history's most costly natural disaster was casually recorded as TD-3—tropical depression number three.

August 16 was a Sunday, a day when the National Weather Service allows itself to reduce forces and ease up the tension as long as there are no threats on the distant horizon. The storm called TD-3 was tracked only through satellite observation, and so when the first reconnaissance flight entered the wall of TD-3 early Monday morning, the one-day lapse in close-hand surveillance brought a surprise. By 8 a.m. August 17, Andrew had earned his name as the Western Hemisphere's first tropical storm of 1992. As is the protocol when a tropical storm is on the map, the National Hurricane Center began holding daily conferences at 7:30 a.m., during which the overnight data were assimilated and the reports of the reconnaissance flights were promptly evaluated.

Two days later, by the morning of Wednesday, August 19, Andrew had spun its way across 15 degrees of longitude, heading generally west/northwest on a traditional course that could eventually threaten the Dominican Republic. But that day the morning flight into Andrew found a surprise. Instead of a slowly growing tropical storm, it found an air mass in disarray, battered by a rival weather system on its way to England. The center of the air mass was not well defined, its forward motion seemed to have slowed, and the sustained wind speed was down. To hopeful observers, Andrew appeared to be on the verge of dying.

Limited in its ability to survey the entire storm because of its slow, low-flying, propeller-driven aircraft, the hurricane center nevertheless determined that Andrew had been decapitated by the more powerful weather system that was heading northeast. The P-3 Orion and C-130 aircraft that are used as hurricane hunters are too slow to cover much area and are limited in their ability to fly above a storm to altitudes of between 6 and 10 miles, where jet aircraft can easily maneuver. Although the planes could not fly high enough to make a positive determination, the forecasters decided the England-bound weather system had trimmed the tops from Andrew's storm clouds, dramatically reducing its ability to generate energy. From the data on steering currents that the hurricane-hunter aircraft were able to gather, it seemed Andrew would ultimately blow itself out in a northeasterly swing away from the mainland, repelled, eventually, by the Bermuda high. In truth, as it turned out, Andrew was merely catching its breath.

As Andrew wobbled on a more northerly course, its winds diminishing, a decision was made not to fly into the storm until dawn on Friday, August 21. Once again Andrew surprised the weather aviators. Andrew had traveled across less than 15 degrees of latitude and about the same distance of longitude. Sitting virtually still for several hours, the storm had conserved its energy while drawing strength from the warm ocean currents. It had redefined itself. When the surveillance aircraft arrived that morning, Andrew was in motion again, organized and showing every sign of growing to hurricane status.

At the National Hurricane Center in Coral Gables, director Robert Sheets poured over the masses of data transmitted by the plane and the weather satellites. Andrew had indeed grown stronger, its pressure gradient deepening. The slow-moving planes had detected significant changes in pressure and velocity. But subtle changes were harder to register, and the comparative data that were missing because there had been no direct observations and measurements on Thursday made it all the more difficult to calculate a predicted course. It would take more information than the 8 a.m. Friday flight to accurately predict how rapidly growth would occur or what direction the storm would take.

Nevertheless, the State of Florida Emergency Operations Center (EOC) had opened on Thursday with four staff members working on computer models. Representatives of the Federal Emergency Management Agency (FEMA) visited the state office in Tallahassee to check on the preliminaries. At that time, Andrew seemed to be on a north-by-northwest course that would probably take it into the Middle Atlantic States in the next five or six days at its current course and speed. Normally hurricane watches are posted a minimum of 36 hours before a storm can possibly strike the target area. Warnings usually go up 24 hours in advance of a predicted landfall. There were days left for preparation, if all went as it seemed it would.

During his regular session with emergency preparedness officials on Friday, August 21, Sheets told his counterparts that he had decided that Andrew posed no immediate threat to the Bahamas, Florida, or the rest of the U.S. mainland over the weekend. "'Have a nice weekend,' I told them," he recalled. "But I added, to cover myself, that they better check back with me on Sunday, just in case." The state Division of Emergency Management took the hurricane center at it word. And when Kate Hale, director of the Dade County Office of Emergency Management (OEM), contacted her counterparts in Tallahassee, they told her not to worry and to have a nice weekend, as they planned to do with their first-ever division picnic.

Florida Power and Light Company (FP&L) is one of several corporations and agencies that conduct their own meteorological analyses and come to their own conclusions, often different or earlier than the National Weather Service. With an area of vulnerability extending from Jacksonville to South Dade and including several nuclear reactors, FP&L looks at the foul weather picture on a large scale. According to Robert Marshall, the FP&L vice president in charge of power distribution, it was clear to FP&L on Thursday that the storm would hit in Florida somewhere within the power company's service boundaries.

The need for rapid deployment of repair crews immediately after a storm is as critical as is the need for emergency medical personnel. It was clear that some area of Florida would be affected, and it was known that mobilization would take time. But FP&L and the other power companies in the Southeast had established a protocol whose underlying premise was the agreement that no one would be criticized for crying wolf. When it came to preparedness, they believed it was better to have the help and not need it, than to need it and not have it. So the power companies began preparations for repairing hurricane damage four days before it could possibly be necessary.

Hospitals and health care delivery systems, on the other hand, typically wait until a hurricane watch is issued before they institute emergency plans. They wait until a hurricane warning to act. This means they have no more than 24 hours to execute those plans. Furthermore, hospitals do not have established relationships with hospitals at remote distances as the power companies have, in case the devastation is widespread. Hospitals rely on the next hospital, figuratively just down the street—as if a powerful storm would spare one and take the other. Their plans are based on the false supposition that the hospital will survive without being victimized itself and will only have to cope with casualties from beyond the hospital community. The plans anticipate an extraordinary patient load and some logistical inconvenience for a few days after the storm. The plans do not contemplate a total lack of power, water, and staff reinforcements. Hospitals do not plan to be victims of a storm, only to care for the victims.

Not so the power company. On Thursday the call went out from Florida Power and Light to other states that were parties to the power companies' mutual aid agreement. The power companies immediately began to rearrange their schedules, stockpile repair material, and assemble the men and women who would be needed to repair the damage and replace the frontline FP&L crews in the critical days immediately after a storm. On Saturday morning, August 22, the FP&L emergency control center was opened in downtown Miami, and the company's five helicopters were sent for shelter to five hangars at Tamiami Airport in South Dade County. They would be needed for damage assessment after the storm. On August 22 South Dade seemed the safest place to store them.

Dr. Sheets later admitted that what happened late Friday took him completely by surprise. Heading north by west, Andrew bumped into the Bermuda high, a large high-pressure cell centered over the island of Bermuda. When the Bermuda high is in place, it either pushes weak storms toward the North Atlantic or propels powerful storms in a more westerly direction, aiming them, in effect, at Central and South Florida. When Andrew bumped into the Bermuda high, the storm made a hard left along the 25th degree line of longitude that pierces the heart of the Bahamas and Key Largo. The hard left suggested a turn for the worse. The turn caught Sheets's attention and raised the prospect, at that moment, that the storm could strike Islamorada in the Florida Keys. Sheets followed the data on Andrew as it was collected on August 21, worried that he had lost a precious forecasting edge.

By the end of the day Friday, it was clear Andrew was picking up speed as it picked up power. Sheets said he knew that he had lost a good deal of preparation time when the storm turned to a more westerly direction. The storm's unexpected two-mile-per-hour acceleration in forward speed cut 24 hours from his forecast time. Soon it would be time to say the awful words and issue a hurricane watch.

Sheets was not yet ready to publicly call for a watch or warning zone with the storm at that distance on a Friday night. But he wanted the key officials to know that a watch was coming soon and a warning would probably follow.

According to Sheets, the cost of implementing a hurricane

watch is measured in tens of millions of dollars to each affected community, not counting lost tourist revenue and spoiled vacations. The storm track projections late Friday had the storm landing anywhere from Cuba to Charlotte, North Carolina. There was only one place the storm would come ashore and one place it would depart. It made no sense to put an area as large as the entire coast of Florida, Georgia, and the Carolinas on the costly course of a hurricane watch.

The target area was narrowed dramatically when the first flight rendezvoused with Andrew Saturday morning, August 22. When the weather service plane arrived at 26.2 degrees latitude and 67.9 degrees longitude, 800 miles east of Miami, Andrew was already a minimal hurricane moving at a remarkable 17 miles an hour. There was little question then that the storm would strike somewhere on the Florida peninsula.

Just to get a firsthand opinion, Kate Hale stopped by the Coral Gables office of the hurricane center that Saturday morning. Sheets confided in her that things looked pretty grim for South Florida. Hale took the warning seriously and began calling in her staff for a 6 p.m. meeting at the Office of Emergency Management bunker in southwest Dade County.

In his hotel room in Puerto Rico, Frank Marks, a meteorologist with the National Oceanic and Atmospheric Administration (NOAA), began to plot the course of Hurricane Andrew. He had just arrived on a flight from Miami, specifically to intercept Andrew. His specialty was measuring storms using airborne Doppler radar, so he was looking forward to flying into Andrew. However, Marks would later confess to newspaper reporters that he was certain, as early as Saturday morning, the storm would strike South Florida. It could go nowhere else, he calculated, because of the directional pressure that was being exerted by the Bermuda high.

Back in Miami, Sheets confronted the familiar problem. To forecast a landfall in South Florida would mean hundreds of millions of dollars in costs for Dade, Broward, and Palm Beach counties. The track into South Florida also would mean warnings for Fort Myers, a watch as far north as Tampa, and watches along a wide area of the Gulf Coast.

At 11 o'clock on Saturday morning, the National Hurricane

Center announced: "Andrew continues to strengthen." Three hours later, with the storm 655 miles east of Miami, it was still not time to make the official call. "The westward movement is expected to continue through Sunday, increasing the threat to South and Central Florida. Interests in that area should closely monitor advisories on this hurricane," the later announcement said.

But the official emergency network personnel got a different message—and not a minute too soon. In Tallahassee, based on the Friday advisories, the state EOC staff went ahead with their planned departmental picnic, held at a park 12 miles from the nearest telephone. In midafternoon a courier was dispatched to find the staff and warn them that the storm was headed for South Florida with increasing speed. Leaving families and picnic baskets behind, the state EOC staff rushed back to the capital. The 27 participating state agencies, the power companies, and Southern Bell were called to the EOC, and operations began in earnest on Saturday night.

At 5:45 p.m., just in time for prime-time newscasts, Sheets decided he could wait no longer. Hurricane watch flags—a black square on a red background—were hoisted from Titusville to Key West. Sheets said that at that moment, 36 hours before the ultimate landfall, the odds were highest—20 percent—that Andrew would come ashore along the Dade-Broward county line. The odds were lower by a few percentage points every 20 miles north and south of the line. The chance of Andrew riding into South Dade and missing the metropolitan areas of Miami Beach and Miami was pretty slim—about 16 percent when the hurricane watch went up.

Stated another way, only 36 hours before South Dade was raked with 170-mile-per-hour winds, suffering $16 billion in damage, its residents were told there was an 84 percent chance the storm would not strike them at all. Fortunately, the area of watch was accurate in its scope, including the area from the Florida Keys northward to Cape Kennedy.

Another fortunate occurrence was the professionalism of Randle-Eastern Ambulance Service. Beginning Saturday morning, the Randle staff reviewed its list of adult congregate living facilities (ACLFs), nursing homes, and other health care facilities for which it had been assigned evacuation responsibilities by the Dade EOC. Patients on ventilators, cardiac monitors, and IVs were first priority, and many were taken to Palm Beach, despite the time it took to make the 140-mile round-trip drive. Ken Randle called each facility on the list to determine if the population had changed or if any other extraordinary changes had occurred since the list was made. For many of the ACLFs, this was their only notification that an evacuation could be imminent.

"We were planning ahead on Saturday because we knew that if it hit, it would be on a Sunday, when management was not around," Randle explained. "We were able to contact the heads of the facilities at their homes. The only problem we had was that the longer you wait, the harder it gets. As it turned out, some of our cars arrived at the facilities unannounced to determine what the needs were."

Among the facilities Randle-Eastern evacuated at the end of the day was Mercy Hospital. According to Randle,

> We were still taking people out of there at eight or nine at night, the night before the storm. To my knowledge, the facilities that we knew about—whether we had contracts with them or not—we went there. It was better to find a place empty than to go there and find someone still in a bed. When we were done we put an ambulance and a fire truck, at least, at every shelter.

When it became clear a big storm was on the horizon, politicians, agency heads, and a state supreme court justice jammed the state EOC. None of them had been involved in any of the preliminary emergency planning sessions, which designated staff representatives had attended. So instead of a trained and disciplined professional staff preparing for the impending disaster, the agency heads and politicians took over, moving the decision-making process from the EOC to the governor's conference room and eliminating the trained EOC agency representatives from the critical processes of decision making and interagency communications.

Later, a local newspaper would lambaste Metro Dade Mayor Steve Clark for staying at home and leaving the job of hurricane evacuation and recovery to the professionals. But as Hurricane Andrew targeted South Florida, the state's emergency professionals were wishing all the politicians would simply stay home. Thirty-six hours before Andrew, the process was already starting to unravel at the most critical points.

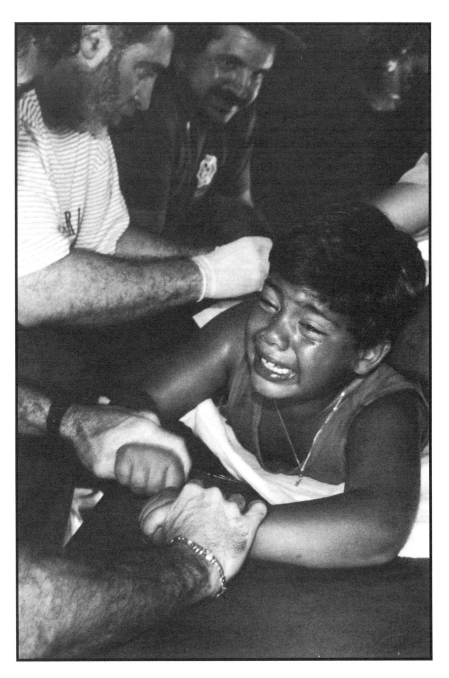

Even minor injuries not directly related to the hurricane—in this instance a leg wound from a bicycle accident—become difficult. A National Guard unit, part of a force of 25,000 troops, erected a field hospital in a driveway, where 300 patients were quickly treated for dehydration, cuts, puncture wounds, and rashes in the days following Andrew.

2

A RACE AGAINST TIME

Emergency agencies, relief agencies, and health care agencies in South Florida, like those in most other hurricane-prone areas, do not begin formal preparations for a severe storm until they hear the gong. When all goes well, the alarm—the hurricane watch—sounds as much as 36 hours before actual landfall. At this point most hospitals begin to begin their hurricane plans. Most other medical facilities go to a state of alert and locate their key staff members. All of them begin to contact the emergency management offices in their area. But little else that involves extra staffing and additional expenditure is done until a hurricane warning is issued. In most cases, that alarm is sounded at least 24 hours before the first effects of the storm are expected to arrive. Because of liability issues, the EOCs, as a matter of policy, do not issue a mandatory evacuation order until the hurricane warning flags fly.

For the individual homeowner, the typical citizen, 24 hours is enough time to prepare the home and to shop and secure emergency supplies not already on hand. But the evidence shows that it is rarely enough time to prepare all the components of the health care delivery system for a major disaster such as a Category 3 hurricane. ("Category 3" is a meteorological classification indicating winds ranging from 111 to 130 miles per hour.)

In South Florida, for example, along the projected path of Hurricane Andrew at the moment of hurricane watch, there were 308 adult congregate living facilities and 91 hospitals. At least

1,700 individuals with special needs had asked Dade County to evacuate them to a shelter. Another 6,000 residents of Miami Beach, most of them elderly, would need assistance in evacuation. Four hospitals were located near enough to the ocean to make wave damage, storm surge, or flooding a potential hazard. The hospitals facing a forced evacuation for a Category 3 storm included Miami Heart Institute North and South, Mt. Sinai Hospital, and South Shore Hospital. Hospitals facing forced evacuation at the next-higher storm level, Category 4, were Victoria Hospital and Mercy Hospital. Those hospitals that would be ordered to evacuate under the highest storm level, Category 5, included Grant Center, Harbor View Hospital, Aventura Hospital and Health Center, and South Miami Hospital at Homestead. Literally dozens of adult congregate living facilities were built in the flood plain or along the shore. Also at risk were hundreds of pharmacies, ambulatory clinics, physicians' offices, HMOs, and rehabilitative centers.

The demands on the health care community for the evacuation of facilities and the relocation of patients far exceeded the ability to respond, despite statutory requirements that hurricane plans include specific measures to take care of special-needs individuals at home and in medical facilities. When Hurricane David threatened Miami in 1979, the Dade evacuation plan had put Miami Beach's elderly in a shelter at the Miami Beach Convention Center, rather than moving them inland. The convention hall was filled with 6,000 mostly frail and elderly, with virtually no medical assistance.

Florida state law requires that all hospitals institute and follow a hurricane plan. It requires the same of nursing homes. And because of the 1979 debacle, Florida law thereafter required that special-needs individuals be offered the opportunity to be listed on a registry so they could be contacted and evacuated to shelter after a hurricane warning is sounded.

According to Alan Clive, the civil rights program manager for FEMA, Dade County registered 1,700 special-needs patients in 1992. Clive said that Kate Hale, the Dade emergency management coordinator, estimated there were 10,000 special-needs clients in the county who could have used help at the time of Andrew. Others have put the number at 50,000, using standard measures of disability. Groups representing the aged note that

380,000 Dade residents are over the age of 60. Many of them were, at the time of Andrew, frail enough to need help.

The implication for the future of special-needs evacuation is critical. Assuming the elderly population survives at existing mortality rates, Dade will have at least 150,000 frail elderly in less than 10 years. And with the growing popularity of coastal cities as retirement havens, the problems of evacuating frail elderly multiply with each passing year in the sunny counties of Florida, the Gulf Coast, and the southeast coast of the United States.

According to the experts, if all the resources of the emergency medical transportation network had been employed to transport to shelters or hospitals everyone in the hurricane watch area who could meet some criteria for special needs, the effort could have taken a week. But no one, under the current method of planning, enjoys the luxury of time to implement an elaborate plan, or the luxury of clear roads to travel and low-stress participants. Everyone in the health care network waits for the hurricane watch to begin staging, and everyone waits until the warning to begin action.

Worse yet, this two-day window of opportunity inevitably occurs at the exact time the rest of the community is involved in its own chaotic preparations, taxing every aspect of the infrastructure, slowing traffic, reducing the availability of all manpower at the moment it is needed most, and making intense, competing demands on stressed emergency personnel. The result is a highly inefficient collision of priorities.

As Andrew approached, the evacuation of special-needs individuals to shelters was a high priority, reinforced by state law. The goal was to get the frail elderly, ventilator patients, dialysis patients, and blind, retarded, or psychiatric patients relocated out of the storm's path to places where they were not only safe from wind and water but able to receive the constant attention many of them needed. At the same time, three hospitals in Miami Beach and one in Miami were ordered to be totally evacuated of patients who were too sick to be sent home. These hospitals did not evacuate voluntarily and, in at least one case, waited until the last minute before obeying the order to depart. Likewise hundreds of nursing home patients were housed in evacuation areas, while hundreds of other people who relied on life support equipment that needed dependable power were also scheduled for evacuation—but not until the announcement of a mandatory evacuation after the announcement of the hurricane warning.

Many of the ACLFs, nursing homes, and hospitals had made arrangements with Medi-Car Systems of Miami or Randle-Eastern Ambulance Service to bring their patients to shelter or move them to another hospital. Others relied on a system of school buses and Metro Dade Transit buses that had been established by and was directed by Dade County's Office of Emergency Management. If health care facilities had begun their evacuation at the hurricane watch or earlier, they might have been able to retain some control over the process and the transportation vendors. As it turned out, according to Sara Grim, president of the South Florida Hospital Association, 1,500 hospital patients were successfully evacuated, but another 500 could not be evacuated due to an inadequate supply of transportation resources.

Michele Baker is the emergency management director for Pasco County, Florida. Until the 1993 hurricane season she had spent seven years as the Dade County hurricane coordinator, working for Kate Hale. Baker was responsible for the special-needs component during Hurricane Andrew, and her story is one of pulling success from the jaws of the defeat that had occurred 13 years earlier. "In 1979, when Hurricane David threatened Miami," she recalled, "Dade County evacuated 6,000 frail, medically needy elderly people to the convention center with absolutely no staff to help them."

The Florida legislature reacted to this nightmare by passing the bill that required emergency management organizations at the county level to voluntarily register anyone who needs assistance in order to evacuate. Registration is not required for the truly needy. The county is not required to perform any outreach, to keep complete records, or to have a program in place to support the effort. The state provides no money to pay for the registry or the transportation, Baker said.

For the first six years after Hurricane David there was no plan for special-needs individuals. Their names were kept on file cards in a file box, according to Baker. "The plan was, I guess, that if a hurricane came I would go out and take the file box and pick them up."

As the elderly became more activist, concurrent with the

development of elderly affairs programs and centers on aging at the universities, Florida International University began to collect information on special-needs individuals by, in Baker's words, "pilfering other data bases and programs."

As the system was developed, registration of special-needs individuals was done through self-addressed, stamped envelopes included in information packets that county officials would hand out whenever they spoke on hurricane preparedness. Registration forms were also distributed through certain health care providers, such as home health agencies, and were included once a year in Florida Power and Light bills.

Baker suggests that the registration information submitted by special-needs individuals should always include whether the individual is coming to the shelter with a care giver or other people. "On several occasions, when we went to pick people up, we ended up with eight of them—someone who was sick and did not have a car and the rest of the family along for the ride," Baker recalled. She said the registration information also should include a signature of the individual to be evacuated, since well-meaning neighbors or relatives could sign up a special-needs individual who is not aware of the program, creating a controversy.

Baker said there is a continual controversy over the request that the patient's physician fill out a section of the registry. One problem is that some people do not meet the requirements for special needs, and their doctors might say so. Others do not wish to spend the money for a doctor visit. Others do not want anyone to know the severity of their disability for fear they will become victims of robbery or worse should the file become public.

Baker said the effort to gain more information is actually a ruse. "We really cannot require them to provide anything more than their name or their address. Anything else we get is gravy," she said. "If they fall for it and the doctor fills it out, we have better information."

In Dade County, the special-needs evacuation program was not on the county's priority list for data base development. Baker and the emergency planners wrote a program of their own and manually entered the list, which was continually updated but was not culled for deaths. It was purged once a year. People who continued to respond each year remained in the file. Those who missed three consecutive years, for whatever reason, were dropped from the service. The notice sent in the third year after the special-needs person failed to respond included a warning that the person would be dropped if no response was forthcoming, according to Baker. This was designed to scare people into responding.

Likewise, Baker said, she developed a release form to be signed by special-needs registrants who decided they did not want to go to a shelter. To frighten the citizen into submitting to the evacuation, the form raised the specter of death and the notification of the next of kin. "As they learned in Hurricane Camille, asking people for their next of kin is often sufficient to scare them into doing what is right," she said.

In Broward County, however, the situation was different. As a matter of county policy, the neediest among the special-needs patients were barred from the special-needs shelters. As reflected in the Hollywood Memorial Hospital emergency plan, the eligibility requirements for the county's three special emergency shelters precluded the following:

1. Patients who are not ambulatory.
2. Wheelchair patients who cannot transfer from wheelchair to bed or toilet without assistance.
3. Patients who require 24-hour electrical power for their treatment modality.
4. Patients who are incontinent of stool or urine.
5. Patients who have advanced Alzheimer's not accompanied by care giver or companion.
6. Patients with early Alzheimer's, not accompanied by care giver or companion.
7. Patients who are confused and not oriented to their own identity.
8. Patients who are psychotic/schizophrenic.

The shelters were allowed to accept the following:

1. Persons who need assistance to administer their own injectable medications.
2. Persons who need assistance with ostomy management and catheters.
3. Persons with minimal restrictions in performing activities of daily living (need little or no supervision from medical personnel).

4. Persons who require minimal monitoring of an unstable medical condition.
5. Persons who need intermittent use of oxygen.

One hospital that thoroughly planned for the evacuation was Mercy Hospital, a 512-bed, acute-care hospital built on the shores of Biscayne Bay along a low-lying section of South Miami Avenue, just north and east of the commercial heart of Coconut Grove. The Mercy Hospital emergency plan, approved in 1990, is predicated on the amount of flooding the hospital is expected to endure, even though the hospital is in a mandatory evacuation zone because it is on low ground, virtually at the water's edge.

The Mercy Hospital hurricane plan assumes that the hospital will be flooded in all storm scenarios, and it establishes different protocols for various water depths. The plan assumes that the Mercy Professional Building and Mercy Outpatient Center will be inaccessible by car for 24 hours and without water for 48 hours at a minimum. Tenants in the office building are expected to secure their own offices, then leave the area until the waters recede.

The plan for the hospital building contemplates a partial evacuation of the building and a total evacuation of the first floor in a minimal storm. Beyond that, the emergency plan for Mercy is a plan for total evacuation. The hospital integrated its emergency plan so that every service and staff member knows what is expected at every stage of the process, from prestorm stockpiling through poststorm insurance settlements.

With a patient population of 240 on the morning of Saturday, August 22, Mercy Hospital president Ed Rosasco—the only hospital official empowered to order an evacuation under the Mercy plan—decided there was no need to wait for the weather forecaster's warning to evacuate the potential storm surge area. Those patients who could be sent home were discharged. The others were to be disbursed among 11 other hospitals in the area.

In 1990, Mercy Hospital had established a contract for evacuation transportation with Medi-Car Systems of Miami, one of two primary medical transport contractors for Metro Dade County. The agreement said that after Medi-Car completed its contractual responsibilities for evacuating patients residing in county-operated facilities, it would take care of Mercy's needs "by assigning all other available vehicles to the facility." In addition, Medi-Car agreed to assign an employee as coordinator of transportation. It agreed to transport not only the patient but the patient's wheelchair or walker and other personal necessities. It agreed to bill Mercy for the service at the customary rates. Mercy agreed to pay within 30 days.

Mercy also agreed to put identification bracelets on each patient that included their shelter destination. No provision was written in the contract for communicating the level of care that the individual patients needed. Nor was there a legal agreement to assure that the Medi-Car staff would transmit critical information to the staff at the receiving hospital about the patient's history and medication needs. There were no provisions for what the driver should do if the designated hospital was filled to capacity, closed, or unwilling to take the patient. The contract included no discussion of liability.

In October 1990, Mercy had established a contractual relationship with six hospitals in the area to accept patients in the event of an emergency. Those hospitals were AMI Kendall Regional Medical Center, Doctors Hospital, North Gables Hospital, Coral Gables Hospital, South Miami Hospital, and Parkway Regional Medical Center. Each of the six contracts is identical in content. They provide a model for other facilities that might face a similar situation. The salient points of the contract are listed here:

1. The affected facility (sending facility) shall notify the other facility (receiving facility) of the disaster and its intent to act upon this agreement prior to implementing any transfers, and

2. The receiving facility shall indicate the number of patient beds available for the receipt of such transferred patients and identify the type of patients that can be accommodated (i.e. intensive care, obstetrics, etc.) and

3. Prior to transferring a patient, the transferring facility must receive confirmation from the receiving facility that it can, in fact, accept the patient, and

4. It shall be the responsibility of the transferring facility to arrange and provide for transport of a patient to the receiving facility and to provide, if necessary, proper medical support during transport, and

5. The medical record (medical and financial/demographic) will accompany each transferred patient at the time of transfer, and

6. It shall be the responsibility of the sending facility to endeavor to meet the staffing needs of the receiving facility to the extent requested by the receiving facility for the proper care of the transferred patient, and

7. In the event the attending physician of a transferred patient is not on the medical staff of the receiving facility, and in the event said physician wishes to continue attending to his patient at the receiving facility, the receiving facility agrees to the patient's third party and personal payments, and

8. In the event the transferred patient's attending physician does not desire or otherwise is not able to obtain such emergency temporary privileges, the receiving facility shall arrange for the assignment of an appropriate physician to the patient, and

9. Patient valuables of any transferred patient that have been placed in the sending facility's safe prior to the transfer shall remain there notwithstanding the transfer of the patient. Patient valuables in the possession of the patient at the time of transfer shall be the responsibility of the patient and/or the sending facility, and

10. Transferred patients will be returned to the sending facility as soon as it is able to provide for their care, subject to the patient's medical condition permitting. It shall be the responsibility of the sending facility to provide transport for the return of such patients, and

11. The sending facility will assume financial responsibility for any non-insured patients who are transferred as the result of this agreement and shall be responsible, within 30 days of receipt of a statement from the receiving facility, for paying such bills, and

12. For insured patients, the receiving facility agrees to accept the patient's third party and personal payments, and

13. In the event the transferred patient is an HMO or other contractually provided patient whose carrier does not recognize the receiving facility, thereby refusing to tender payment, the sending facility will be financially responsible to the receiving facility for the cost of the patient's care and treatment. Each facility agrees to honor the other's contractually negotiated rates for patients so transferred, and

14. This agreement shall be effective as of the date indicated

and shall remain effective for an indefinite period of time. Either party may terminate this agreement without cause upon giving not less than 30 days prior written notice, providing that any patient still in the receiving facility at the time of termination shall continue to be classified as a transferred patient under this agreement as if the agreement were still in force, and

15. It is further agreed between the parties that transfer shall be limited by the receiving facility's ability to provide care for such inpatients and that the agreement does not supersede either facility's rights and obligations under COBRA, OBRA, and/or Florida Statutes and Rules and Regulations regarding patient dumping.

Regardless of the facilities' plans, when the warning is sounded in Dade County (and most other counties), the county emergency planners take control of the ambulances and dispatch them according to their priorities. Therefore, valid emergency plans can become barriers to implementing other valid emergency plans unless a comprehensive approach is taken.

What the winds do not destroy, rains can turn into a waterlogged mess. The glowering clouds bringing unwanted rain and the high winds lashing the landscape only spell more trouble for struggling survivors as a tarp is hurriedly spread over a roofless house in Homestead. Midweek there were still 420,000 homes and businesses without electricity.

WHEN PLANS MEET REALITY

The telephone bank, the most critical component of the Dade County Emergency Operations Center, was designed to fail. A dozen different emergency functions—including a two-line computer notifier system for special-needs citizens, communications and dispatch for police, dispatch for fire rescue and the National Guard, rumor control, and the 911 system for Dade County—were all on the same rotary phone switches, according to former Dade hurricane coordinator Michele Baker.

As soon as the hurricane watch was posted at 5:45 p.m. on Saturday, August 22, the volume of incoming calls jammed the lines, and the phones did not stop ringing for the next week. Because of the failure to plan for the volume of calls, during the first few critical days of operation (the day before the storm and two days after) it was impossible to make an outgoing call without several failed attempts. The volume of incoming calls also caused the switch to roll over and crash the 911 system, Baker recalled. The poorly planned phone system meant that no one could call into the Emergency Operations Center to report on needs, to request assistance, or to find out where to go with critically needed supplies and volunteers after the storm. "You could not get an outgoing call out of the Dade County EOC for three or four days unless you were persistent and kept dialing over and over again," Baker recounted.

The descent into disorder at the EOC began on Friday, the day before the watch. On that day, relying on information provided by the National Hurricane Center in Coral Gables, the Dade EOC called all the key department heads and agency contacts and told them to monitor the storm. They were told the storm might arrive the next week and some evacuations might be necessary. The implication was strong that they would not be called into action over the weekend. But on Saturday morning, when Kate Hale visited the hurricane center, she was told that things looked pretty grim. The storm had picked up speed and power and was heading for South Florida.

Hale decided not to wait for a hurricane watch to assemble her staff, and she summoned them to the EOC. Most of them arrived before 6 p.m. Saturday, just in time to hear that a hurricane watch had been posted for the area.

Baker recalled the moment. "When the watch went up, the phones went nuts, so there was no ability for any of us to do the kind of build-up that we all had in our plans, the kind of time that we expect to have those first few minutes to get organized and to make our notifications. The storm just picked up speed too fast."

Instead of staying overnight and getting caught up on the preliminaries, most of the EOC staff went home to get sleep and prepare their own families. Baker was among the few who stayed. She worked through the night printing out the schedules and routes for the Metro Dade Transit bus drivers, and for the ambulances and Dade County School District buses that would be used in the evacuation of special-needs patients and other citizens.

Metro Transit personnel arrived at 3 a.m. Sunday morning to get their routes and instructions and begin the process of evacuation. Baker had printed out the list of people in need of evacuation based on the assumption that the storm would reach Category 5, even though Andrew had been a Category 3 storm when she began the process. But by the time the list was finished, the storm had grown to Category 4 strength, so evacuation level E, the maximum evacuation plan, was the correct protocol.

If Baker had not stayed, or if she had printed a list for evacuation based only on a Category 3 storm, the evacuation process would have been set back by four or five hours and probably never completed. As it was, bus drivers were still picking up elderly individuals and carrying them down stairs from their apartments and condos at 12:30 a.m. Monday, with the wind whistling around them and sand blowing in their faces, two hours before the hurricane winds arrived.

At 3 p.m. on Sunday, the afternoon before the storm, 12 hours before local winds reached hurricane speed, only 10 percent of the special-needs individuals had been transported. The Metro buses, which had been detailed to carry wheelchair patients, could carry only two or three patients in chairs at a time. Special transportation services were so overwhelmed with their regular clients they were unable to help. And the school buses with special lifts for wheelchair patients were late to arrive and early to leave.

When the school board transportation officials were notified that they would be needed, they realized they had no system to notify the school board officials who had the authority to mobilize the drivers. Because it was a weekend and no one had home phone numbers, the transportation administrator at the school board was not notified until 1 p.m. Sunday, four hours after the hurricane warning. The first school bus did not arrive until 2:30 p.m.

As a result of this experience with Hurricane Andrew, Florida Department of Transportation (DOT) employees and those of several businesses that must react to an impending storm have since organized to eliminate this problem of notification. This is a lesson that might be learned by all agencies that have employees who must be contacted before or after a storm. The DOT employees are told well in advance where they are to be and when they are to be there. They are assigned a vehicle and a task, so that there is no need for anyone in management to contact them to get them started on their important tasks. They also know how long they are expected to work and where they are supposed to report during work and once their tour of duty is completed.

This was not the case with the school bus drivers before Hurricane Andrew. They did not show up until they were told to show up, and they were not told how long they were expected to work. Around 7 p.m., with thousands yet to be evacuated, the school bus drivers decided it was too dangerous to work and went home, leaving the Metro buses and the ambulances to finish the evacuation. "The Metro bus drivers went so far beyond the call of duty," Baker raved. "Their responsibility was to merely go to the curb and stop and wait. But they did much more. They drove, they stopped. Where the power had gone out, they climbed the stairs and carried people and their baggage down. They picked up people in stretchers and just laid them on the floor. What these guys did was just incredible. They didn't have to do it, but they did," Baker recalled.

At Mercy Hospital, despite all the preplanning for evacuation, things were not going as smoothly as hoped. Medi-Car, the ambulance service that had contracted with Mercy to evacuate its advanced life-support patients, was inundated with requests for transport from its various clients and others as well. The demands quickly exceeded the ability to respond, so Medi-Car dispatchers set their own priorities based on efficiency and the distances to be traveled. This left Mercy at the mercy of chance when it came to the timing of its evacuation.

Carlos Blanco, a manager at Medi-Car who was on duty at the time of the evacuation, recalled,

> Dade County did not take command of our vehicles. We set the priorities for the use of our vehicles by location and how many patients they had, and we did our evacuation following that priority. We tried to get everything on the beach and on the coast out first, and from there we tried to work inland. We did not have actual contracts other than Mercy. The ones who called us at the time were the ones we evacuated. Everybody that called us, we did evacuate. We started at five in the morning and didn't finish until midnight on the day of the storm. They went everywhere. You name it, they went there, mostly other hospitals and other nursing homes. Some went to hospitals up in Broward. It was a crazy time. Every vehicle we have, 28 units, was involved in it. If there was a call for an ambulance at the time, we would pull one of the vehicles off the evacuation to handle it. . . .
>
> If there was one thing we learned, it was that evacuations have to start earlier. It did not really make any difference if anyone had a contract at that time. Those people we did a lot of business with, we tried to accommodate them more rapidly. It gets to a point where contracts really don't count. The bottom line was, we didn't care who you were, we were going to move it.

The movement of patients among the hospitals was complicated by the fact that those hospitals that had formal agreements with other hospitals to take patients were also asked to take patients from hospitals with which they had no formal agreements. Agreements hospitals had made with other hospitals to take patients in case of evacuation did not anticipate the demand that would be placed on them to take patients from facilities that had been ordered to evacuate. Mercy found accommodations for its final four patients at Deering Hospital in South Dade at 6 p.m. Sunday, just hours before the winds began to blow. As it turned out, those patients were in for the time of their lives.

As the storm approached the Florida peninsula, the reports from the Bahamas were chilling. The wind was clocked at 150 miles an hour, sustained, at 2 p.m. Sunday afternoon. In Miami the wind was still a breeze, and a fiercely hot sun beat down on those making last-minute modifications to their homes and places of work.

At the region's 79 movable bridges, Florida Department of Transportation crews stood by, awaiting orders to lock them down, preventing passage by boats and thereby facilitating evacuation. (State law says that all bridges under the control of the DOT are to be locked down when the wind reaches 39 miles an hour. But the law does not say *where* the wind must reach 39 miles an hour. State law does not say *how long* the wind must blow 39 miles an hour. Nor does it say *who* decides that the wind has reached the required level or who makes the announcement.) In the meantime, the bridges, over which a massive evacuation was being conducted, opened and shut on the demand of hundreds of boaters attempting to move their craft to safety.

Because Andrew had a smaller diameter than most storms, its 39-mile-per-hour winds did not arrive until the storm was almost on top of Florida. The winds did not reach 39 miles an hour when expected, and the evacuation of the coastal areas was hampered by the constant raising of the bridges to allow pleasure craft to venture inland for protection.

Meanwhile, 517,000 residents from the Keys and the mandatory evacuation zones, as well as other area residents who did not feel safe at home, clogged the mainland highway system. No one expected the volume of traffic or the amount of impedance automatic toll booths might cause. Traffic backed up for miles as families who were fleeing for their lives fumbled for quarters at the toll plazas and fumed that the state could be so stupid and greedy. It took a televised complaint from a local weather reporter for the state to realize that taking tolls along the turnpike system meant risking the lives of thousands of evacuees. Long after the decision should have been made, the toll booths were opened for unfettered passage.

At 7 p.m. no one was officially allowed across the causeways onto Miami Beach. This meant that the thousands of elderly residents who remained in their condominiums, unwilling or unable to evacuate, could not be reached by their children or friends, and their only hope was an official evacuation vehicle.

Since the phones had jammed at the EOC immediately after the hurricane watch was sounded, the EOC was not able to make phone calls and warn special-needs individuals to pack and eat a meal and await further notice. Likewise, when the evacuation order came at 9 a.m. on Sunday, the EOC was not able to notify special-needs patients that someone would be coming within six hours, as prescribed in the emergency management hurricane plan.

Metro Dade Fire Rescue, which includes the Metro Dade Fire Department (MDFD) and its rescue component, went on alert, like the other government agencies, when the watch was sounded at 5:45 p.m. on Saturday, August 22. Metro Dade Fire Rescue is the heart of the emergency medical system in Dade County, since it serves all of unincorporated Dade and 22 incorporated municipalities, with 1,400 uniformed personnel at a total of 40 stations. It is an experienced unit that includes a special team of urban rescue workers who have flown around the world to locate and treat the injured in the aftermath of natural disasters.

Fire Rescue's communication system links its fleet of vehicles to the area's hospitals through the Medcom radio network, with eight dedicated radio frequencies. On most occasions, basic life support transports are hired out to commercial ambulance companies, including Randle-Eastern Ambulance Service and Medi-Car. Advanced life support missions are handled exclusively by Fire Rescue's 30 ground rescue units and two Bell 412 helicopters.

Unlike the Metro Dade Police, Metro Dade Fire Rescue took down its tallest antennas before the storm and operated with shorter transmission units. After the storm, the masts were reinstalled, along with portable repeaters at strategic locations to complete a fairly resilient communications network. Unfortunately, no other agency had equipment that could tap into the fire and rescue bands.

The unionized fire fighters had developed strict and clear-cut rules about who comes and who goes when a hurricane watch turns into a warning. The strengths and weaknesses of these specific policies are worth considering by other groups. The MDFD After Action Report tells the story as only an official fire department report can:

> Upon announcement of the hurricane watch, all essential MDFD personnel were placed on standby status and . . . were expected to take immediate steps to secure their property and family.
>
> Upon announcement of a hurricane warning, the normal complement of on-duty operations personnel will be augmented by the immediate past shift. Unless otherwise instructed, on-coming personnel are expected to report to their duty station within one hour after the hurricane warning is announced. On-duty personnel will be relieved of duty by the reporting immediate past shift in order to secure their property and family prior to reporting back to duty. Employees are expected to return to their duty stations within 4 hours.
>
> Since the warning occurred right at shift change (7 a.m.), it was difficult to determine who was the "immediate past shift." The off-going shift (immediate past shift) had not had the opportunity to secure their property and families. This led to many more people than planned needing to be off to secure personal business.

The bad timing aside, the fire fighters have learned over the years that they get more out of their personnel if they allow everyone to have time to prepare their own home before the storm and time for them to return home as soon as possible after the storm.

At Florida Power and Light, the employees on duty during an emergency are also assured that someone in the system will attempt to locate their family. They are assured that housing will be provided if needed and loans will be available on demand. This dramatically reduces the stress on the first wave of emergency repair workers and would be an excellent policy for health care personnel who must be on duty immediately before, during, and after a storm.

At 7:30 p.m. on Saturday, Fort Lauderdale International Airport closed. At 9:30 p.m. Miami International Airport closed. The two closures stranded hundreds of tourists who had been forced out of their hotel rooms as most of the beachfront hotels decided to heed the evacuation order.

The situation was especially chaotic at certain locations. At the Fountainbleu Hotel, for example, the majority of the guests were European. Few spoke enough English to understand what to do or where to go when the instructions were broadcast. Few paid attention to the increasingly alarming weather forecasts until the hotel told them they must leave and should not expect to find rooms south of Orlando. The guests at the Fountainbleu ultimately were forced from their rooms and told the location of hurricane shelters. Many fled to the airport in a vain attempt to catch a flight anywhere. Most of them weathered the blow at the airport.

The deaf and hearing impaired were worse off than the non–English-speaking Europeans. The Federal Communications Commission requires that all emergency information be provided over television in the form of a "crawler," a written message to accompany any voice message and pictures. The crawler moves across the bottom of the screen to inform the hearing impaired of what is happening and to tell them what to do when a broadcast is not closed-captioned and no one is available to sign.

Tyrone Kennedy, the founder of the Deaf Services Bureau in Dade County, recalls that the system worked well until the hurricane watch was changed to a hurricane warning. At that moment his 30,000 clients who relied entirely on signing or closed captioning were spread throughout Dade County. An equal number in Broward and Palm Beach counties were also left to wonder if they were going to be targets of the worst part of the storm and if they were expected to evacuate.

At the moment of greatest need, the television stations stopped using the crawler because the emergency messages were too long, complicated, and varied to be reduced to writing. "Once it changed from the watch to a warning we lost it all. The deaf population had no knowledge of what was going on. They missed out completely," according to Kennedy. He continued,

When the warning came, we went into action at Deaf Services. We called the National Hurricane Center to ask them where the interpreter should go, because the interpreter always goes to the National Hurricane Center to be there when the news media come in, so they can show the interpreter along with the announcements of the impending hurricane. That did not happen. We called and I did not get through. When I did, they said they did not need one, if they did they would call me back. I never got the call.

I proceeded then to call all the television stations, because we had a plan to send the interpreters to the stations to meet with a designated person who would bring them into the newsroom where the announcements would be made. None of the television stations were receptive to bringing an interpreter in. It was just a complete failure in trying to get the deaf and the hearing impaired informed. When we finally got through to Channel 10, they said to go ahead and send an interpreter. We sent an interpreter. That was about 10 p.m. that night. By the time those people who would have relied on this information, if it came sooner, found [the station and got the information], by then it was too late. The stores were all empty. There were no supplies left.

After the storm the power breakdown made it impossible to contact the deaf by phone, since their TTY machines required electricity, Kennedy explained. The machines' battery backup is good for a few hours unless the printer is used. In that case the batteries' life is substantially shorter. "So we learned, at least, not to use the printers," he said. Deaf Services then capitalized on telephone technology to solve its communications problems, according to Kennedy. He forwarded all the calls that were directed to Deaf Services to an apartment in North Dade where power remained.

After the storm, the only way to get information about clients in the devastated area was to send staff and volunteers to the clients' last known address. There was no way to call them without power. Southern Bell provided a supply of batteries to replace those that had been expended in the individual TTY units, and the field workers exchanged spent batteries for new ones.

Since Hurricane Andrew, the deaf community has discussed the effectiveness of closed captioning in the emergency environment and is now recommending that all emergency messages be sent in open captioning, as written messages visible to all, at the bottom of television screens, at regularly scheduled intervals.

By 10 p.m. on Sunday, August 23, most of the shelters in South Florida were filled to overflowing, and there was still little tangible indication of the power of the storm that was brewing on the horizon. The fearful winds did not begin until midnight. By that time, the limited order that had prevailed dissolved in the deepening gale.

Mental patients without essential psychotropic drugs or the trained professionals to manage them were dropped in the midst of families taking shelter from the storm. Elderly who had not been moved from their beds in years were loaded on buses and dumped at hospitals, nursing homes, and shelters.

Mark Lichtman, a director at the Miami Jewish Home for the Aging, reported that one of his biggest problems came from Jewish residents in the area who had elderly parents living at home or without assistance. Many of them drove up to the already overcrowded home for the aging and, with no advance warning, dropped off their elderly relatives and then raced out of town or for shelter.

The professional nurses who had been hired to help the needy during the storm showed just as little concern for their responsibilities. Michele Baker, the Dade hurricane coordinator, recalled,

We had a program where we were supposed to have public health nurses at three of the major shelters where we were to bring special-needs people. And Dade County had six contracts with private nursing companies to activate to bring in nurses and LPNs.

We activated the contract. Two of the contract nurses responded and said they would come in. Only one showed up. None of the public health nurses showed up. That left us with about 1,100 on special-needs registry and 6,000 people from Miami Beach who were all frail elderly. We had in the neighborhood of 10,000 people in the shelters who had special needs, and all we had to provide help for them was a paramedic and two emergency medical technicians [EMTs] at each shelter in most cases. But those guys are not trained in hand holding, diaper changing, and geriatric medicine, and they were totally overwhelmed with this task of babysitting, and they were underutilized because they could not be out doing search and rescue.

Our responsibility was to make the arrangements for the staff. I want to tell you, we failed. It was not the fault of the Red Cross. It was ours.

The net effect of the failure of the public health nurses and paid, private-duty nurses to respond as promised was that the EMTs had no relief for two full days. Those who helped in the shelters during the storm were compelled to remain at their stations at the shelters the day after the storm, when they might otherwise have been able to relieve their colleagues who were cutting their way through the rubble looking for the dead and treating the survivors.

Baker said, "We had one whole shift [of EMT personnel] in the shelters, a third of our guys, that was inaccessible to us so that the guys who worked all night and were toast had no relief."

Like punch-drunk fighters, the citizens of South Florida absorbed one blow after another. When the winds died, thunderstorms added to the woes of a stunned county and the destruction of Andrew. But, like Rocky, the people picked themselves up and fought on. At one point, 2,000 Florida Power and Light employees were at work on emergency repairs.

THERE HE BLOWS!

Around 4 a.m. on Monday, August 24, the entire power grid serving South Florida collapsed, plunging four million people into darkness, cutting most of them off from television news reports. Above the Redlands Golf Course, just north of the city of Homestead, the Channel 6 television broadcasting tower was taking a beating. At a height of 1,500 feet and installed with the latest in safety features, it was a key communication link between the Keys, South Dade, and the rest of the world. At least a dozen telephone and radio relay stations were installed on the tower. At around 4:30 a.m., when the units of the Metro Dade County Police Department were ordered to take secure shelter, the mighty tower began to bow in the wind.

At 4:55 a.m. the eye wall of the hurricane reached land just south of Key Biscayne, not far from Mercy Hospital. At 4:57 a.m. a gust that might have been as high as 178 miles per hour raked the National Hurricane Center building near 40th Street off Dixie Highway in Coral Gables, two miles north of South Miami Hospital, one mile east of Doctors Hospital, and two miles west of Mercy Hospital. The center's "hurricane-proof" radar antenna was blown off the top of the building by the gust, leaving the hurricane center virtually blind and deaf. Its rooftop altimeters were also destroyed but remained in place with a final reading of 164 miles an hour.

At 5 a.m., as Andrew's eye wall approached areas farther south, the South Florida Water Management District officers who were monitoring their water level gauges in South Dade got a real surprise. They were remotely monitoring the gauges from the safety of a West Palm Beach bunker, a hundred miles north. One of the remote monitors records the outflow of water from the flood control canal opening into South Biscayne Bay near Saga Bay.

As Andrew surged ashore, the power of the low pressure in advance of the eye wall was clearly visible. With the eye wall minutes away, the gauges showed an incredible canal depth of two feet below sea level. For days prior to the storm, the canals had been wide open to handle the expected flooding, and each showed levels at or above sea level. But the last gasp of Andrew before it came ashore had sucked the water from the bay and the canal and piled it up somewhere offshore against the rushing seas.

A few minutes later the storm surge rose to 19 feet and plunged forward at breakneck speed. It picked up the 114-foot-long, 210-ton freighter *Seaward Explorer,* just off Elliot Key, snapped the hawser that held the *Seaward Explorer* to its storm anchor, submerged Elliot Key, and transported the freighter across Elliot Key.

Gathering speed, the wave and the freighter crossed Biscayne Bay and smashed ashore, the water covering everything that did not stand taller than 25 feet. The *Seaward Explorer* came to rest 200 yards from shore in South Dade, 500 feet from Old Cutler Road, just west of the radically shifting canal flood gate. The crew had no idea the ship was not still miles at sea until the surge receded, leaving it and them high and dry.

At the height of the storm, the massive Channel 6 television tower could no longer withstand the storm's force. Its three-inch-diameter cable snapped with a retort like a mortar round exploding, and it toppled to the ground. An area 350 square miles in size lost a major communication facility as the ensemble of antennas crunched to the ground.

Metro Dade Police regional chief Ben Como recalled that a few of his men in each of the four districts south of South West 8th Street remained on patrol until 4:30 a.m., when they were officially told to take cover. Others had sought out a "secure place" somewhat sooner. Como said the problem was that no one knew which buildings would be secure against Andrew. Most agreed that the aluminum hangars at Tamiami Airport would be secure, and so that's where most of the Metro Dade Police aircraft were stashed.

A platoon of Metro Dade police looking for a secure building in South Dade selected a location also popular with building inspectors—the Don Carter Bowling Palace, off U.S. 1 in far South Dade. At about 4:45 a.m., the roof began to leak water, then air, then wind. As the storm entered the alley, the threat of total collapse was imminent, and the police officers spent a terrifying hour hiding beneath the pool tables as the bowling palace crashed around them.

Things were not much better at the regional police and fire rescue headquarters in Cutler Ridge, according to Como. His office was destroyed and with it, his communication system. The explosive decompression in the regional library next door blew off the roof and sent books careening in the wind, some to be found eventually 40 miles away.

When the Channel 6 television tower buckled, Como was left with no radio. He had several cellular phones, but they were battery powered at best and useless in the jammed airwaves caused by the collapse of the Channel 6 tower and several relay stations. With four districts to control, with 1,100 officers to move, and with incredibly important emergency information to dispense, Como was left with one radio frequency that, unfortunately, matched no other nearby law enforcement station or agency.

Como's own words tell the story best:

[Before the] hurricane we had a staff meeting and decided we needed at least 60 percent of our staff available for the storm. That was accomplished.

Our normal radio communications system went down, and we immediately go to the phones and find out that does not work. So we immediately go to the radio phones. When the Channel 6 tower went down that knocked out our communications. The only communications we had that was generic between all the agencies was an emergency frequency—what we referred to as Channel B. Keep in mind that I had four districts, and three were directly affected. I had to make calls to handle every one from Bird Road south. It was terrible. Once you got south of Kendall, the phone systems were shot, so no one could call in.

We had the one generic phone that went to the Cutler Ridge station.

As soon as the storm passed, we had to be back on what was left of the streets to identify the emergency routes and clear them if they were blocked. We had to communicate this to our officers in the field. A lot of people had to be transported to hospitals right after the storm. Then there was a need to do damage assessment, a critical need to keep control of the streets. I needed to determine the extent of curfew, when and where it would be. Communication was paramount and I had one line.

Como said he made a point of arresting people in the first two hours after the storm, putting them in jail, then using the media to advertise that arrests were being made and suspects were being jailed for looting. A total of 149 persons were arrested during those first two hours.

Como learned an important lesson as a result of the storm:

Several of the things we had done in the past will have to be corrected in the future. One is a correction in the terminology, for law enforcement to find themselves a facility that is "secure." No one in law enforcement has taken the time to define what is a "secure facility." We quickly found that out when almost a platoon of officers selected [the] Don Carter Bowling Alley as a secured structure. They soon found out that it was not secure when they spent a couple of hours beneath the pool tables and we lost a couple of vehicles at that location.

We did disburse our aircraft to Tamiami Airport, but they were crushed. So that left us with the problem of acquiring aircraft. Bell Helicopter provided us loaners pretty quickly, and they became extremely valuable in finding out what happened down south, because they were the only way to transport ourselves.

Reflecting on his experience, Como spoke of the storm with veneration. "Andrew provided an awakening to the degree of power Mother Nature has. No degree of planning could have planned for anything as devastating as this."

That is exactly the way they felt at Baptist Hospital.

Baptist Hospital is a large and successful private institution whose history is deeply intertwined with the upscale community it serves. Millionaire developer Arthur Vining Davis sought to develop his vast holdings among the groves and swamps of South Dade. When he heard of plans to build a private hospital near Jackson Memorial Hospital, he contacted the physicians who were organizing the effort and offered to build them a hospital and an access road in the undeveloped South Dade savanna. He promised them lots of new patients from the residential development he hoped to build along Kendall Drive. His "magnet" hospital became Baptist Hospital. As Davis predicted, the hospital prospered as the Kendall area became a major bedroom community, surrounded by planned developments, apartments, and condominiums.

Baptist is far enough inland that fear of storm surge had never been a concern. Similarly, it is not far enough east to cause much worry about flooding from the shallow water table that underlies the reclaimed swamp. As Hurricane Andrew approached, Baptist was committed to staying open and taking care of its clientele.

Like many other successful hospitals, Baptist was deeply involved in marketing its OB/GYN services and birthing suites. The staff knew what most growing hospitals know: women make the health care decisions, and women will stay with the hospital where they have a happy experience giving birth.

Recent years have brought a baby boom among the affluent of South Florida, with an unusually high percentage of first-time mothers around 40 years of age and able to afford pampering beyond the needs or the means of their younger sisters. Baptist had hundreds of these patients who were faced with a real problem as Andrew approached.

The falling barometric pressure of an approaching tropical storm will often induce labor in women in their third trimester, causing premature births and other complications. Those conditions are difficult enough for a young mother, but particularly so for the older first-time mother.

Outside its maternity operation, much of the surgery done at Baptist Hospital is elective, and elective surgery is rarely scheduled for weekends. On Saturday evening, when television reported there was a good chance the storm would hit Miami, Baptist vice president Lee Huntley contacted the hospital switchboard and told the operators to notify all department heads and managers that there would be a hurricane preparedness meeting the next day at 11 in the morning.

Huntley recognized the possibility that no one would be able to reach the hospital or leave for several hours after the storm, so he ordered two shifts to report by midnight, one to sleep through the storm and the other to work. It never occurred to him (or to any of the hospital administrators at other South Dade hospitals) that most of the staff would be required to remain on duty without relief for 36 hours, or that 500 of the 3,200 employees would go home after the grueling shift only to find that they had no home left. Nor could it have been guessed that 1,500 more employees would have endured devastation just short of total destruction.

Baptist made arrangements with emergency physicians and specialists, including obstetricians, surgeons, cardiologists, a neurosurgeon, and anesthesiologists, to leave their families at home while they remained at the hospital during the hurricane. "Everyone made their phone calls, then went home to prepare their homes as best they could. The scenario was, you said good-bye to your family, then you came back to work. It was a very hard thing to do," Huntley recalled.

Pregnant women who were patients at Baptist were contacted by their doctors and told to endure the storm on campus. Some of these women spread the word to friends who were pregnant but who were not patients at Baptist. So many pregnant women showed up at Baptist in the hours before the storm that they filled the auditorium, then spilled into the hallways, then filled the offices of the Joslin Diabetes Clinic. Hospital staff also reluctantly allowed families of women in need to stay, creating problems with space, nutrition, waste disposal, sanitation, and liability. "No woman was turned away from Baptist Hospital prior to the storm," Huntley recalled.

Baptist was not the only hospital with an anticipated baby boom. Jackson Memorial Hospital is the primary public hospital in a region serving more than a million individuals, many of them refugees and immigrants who speak no English. Jackson and its clinics provide most of the prenatal and OB/GYN resources for these populations. As such, Jackson was confronted with substantial numbers of concerned pregnant women. These women were notified over the region's rock, rhythm and blues, reggae, and rap radio stations to plan a stay at Jackson during the storm if they were either within three weeks of their due date or in the

Jackson OB clinic program and had been told to come to the hospital.

For the most part, they were told to leave their other children, friends, mothers, husbands, and boyfriends at home. But few heeded the message. The air-conditioned and seemingly invincible halls of Jackson seemed a much nicer place to weather a storm than crackerbox apartments, shabby shacks, and crowded homes. And so, as Jackson's staff and physicians scrambled to park their boats, spare cars, and mobile homes in the relative safety of the county lots around Jackson, the indigent flocked to Jackson in every manner of transportation, both public and private. Jackson's plan had called for housing some OB families in Jackson Towers, the residential rehabilitation section of the hospital. But this plan never materialized.

Jackson's hurricane plan was long on delegation. Supervisors were responsible for determining the staff that would be adequate for the emergency and for scheduling them. Food was provided "at prevailing prices" until otherwise authorized by the command post. Only physicians and nurses authorized in advance by the command post were allowed to order food delivered from the cafeteria. All others were required to eat in the cafeteria. The OB patients who were told to report to the hospital were expected to either bring food or pay.

Jackson, like most other hospitals, waits for the hurricane warning bell before beginning preparations in earnest. Staffers were scheduled in three shifts: those scheduled for duty before the storm hit, those scheduled to work during the storm, and those scheduled to work after the storm. Employees scheduled to work before and during the storm were required to be in attendance before the storm. They were not allowed to bring family to the facility except with prior approval or if they could not get to a designated shelter on time.

Those scheduled to relieve the hospital staff members working before and during the storm were advised to arrive at work two hours after the storm passed or as soon as possible thereafter. The Jackson plan called for the employees of the Metro Dade Transit Authority, the Jackson Outpatient Transportation Department, the security department, and the material management department to find their way to their buses and then to several strategic landmarks to pick up Jackson employees needing a ride to work. All this was planned as if the storm would hit everyone but employees of Jackson, as if the roads would remain open countywide and the destruction would not affect the staff. As it turned out, approximately 2,400 of Jackson's 7,000 employees lived in the damaged area. Most of them suffered some storm damage, and 500 were left homeless. Therefore, fewer Jackson employees than expected made it to work as ordered by 8 a.m. Monday.

At 3:30 a.m. Monday, as sustained winds exceeded 50 miles an hour, the incident manager for the Metro Dade Fire Department ordered his men and women to stop responding to new calls. Units on call were ordered to report to the nearest fire station to wait out the storm. Once the order was given, all the 911 dispatcher could do was log a call, take the name, address, and phone number of the caller, and promise help once the storm passed.

At some stations, however, the "no response" order was ignored. Acts of heroism took place that will never be known because they involved the violation of direct orders. Some became known through word-of-mouth—such as that involving an EMT crew that tried for an hour to reach 22-year-old Elaida Vargas. Vargas had come to Miami to have her baby, because the poor can have babies free in America and it was safer than in her native Dominican Republic. At 3 a.m. she called for emergency medical assistance, her head pounding with pain. The storm's winds made it impossible for the EMT crew to reach her, despite heroic attempts, and the crew was recalled. Vargas survived the storm but died at 9:30 a.m., killed by a cerebral hemorrhage. Her unborn baby also died.

Other stories had happier endings. At 4:22 a.m., with hurricane winds howling in the background, emergency medical personnel assigned to the communications center successfully helped a desperate father deliver a baby over the phone.

At 4:27 a.m. all of South Florida went dark.

When dawn broke, a surprised captain found his 210-ton, 110-foot-long steel ship landlocked eight miles from where it had been anchored two miles offshore. Hurricane winds that reached 175 miles per hour created a 12- to 14-foot sea surge that lifted a 2,000-pound anchor as though it were a tea bag and left the ship an unwelcome gift in a stranger's backyard.

5

HANGING ON

As the winds reached their peak velocity, hospitals and shelters all across South Florida were learning a difficult lesson in construction. Virtually all the commercial buildings in South Florida keep their central air-conditioning units or cooling towers on the roof. This is also the preferred location for emergency water supplies and communication equipment. The roof location is preferred over ground level for reasons of aesthetics and to avoid water damage from heavy rain and standing water.

Andrew was not a wet hurricane, but it was intensely windy. And so, all across South Dade, in the path of the 140-mile-per-hour winds, air-conditioning units and antennas became projectiles— similar to the hurricane-proof radar that blew off the top of the building that housed the National Hurricane Center.

Virtually every place where an air-conditioning unit had been attached to a roof, Hurricane Andrew left a gaping hole behind, exposing the facilities to torrential rains and devastating winds. The rains poured in and filled the ceilings, then the walls, ending the usefulness of all electrical and communication equipment located within these areas. The rains turned elevators into wells and stairs into waterfalls.

Most hospitals did not board up or otherwise protect their windows above the first floor. Even before the holes were ripped in the roofs, gusts of wind projected objects through many windows, opening up rooms where patients and care givers were huddled. With every breach, the hospital personnel and their patients were forced to retreat deeper and deeper into their facilities. With the power gone, the retreat was into darkness and a damp, fierce heat. Maintaining septic conditions was impossible, as damp, wind-driven debris invaded every corner.

Baptist Hospital had been building a new facility for the Miami Vascular Institute on the floor above the primary surgical unit. The new construction was ripped apart as the winds peaked, opening holes in the roof of the surgery section, filling the ceiling with water. The surgery staff retreated to one of the few areas of the hospital without windows—one tiny room with no power, no fans, no running water, no air conditioning, and no sanitation—to conduct its business.

Deering Hospital, previously called Coral Reef Hospital, had no formal plan for a direct hit from a hurricane. Recently renamed and taken over by the Columbia Hospital Corporation, Deering was becoming the flagship of Columbia's fleet of hospitals in South Florida. The previous hospital administration had developed a plan for what was then a small and struggling facility. But Columbia was new to the scene, with a unique structure of physician ownership. Its administrators had demonstrated their skill at jump-starting failing hospitals around the country. They were not veterans at diagnosing tropical weather.

As Hurricane Andrew moved closer, the Columbia regional officers acted on the earlier predictions that the storm would come ashore north of its actual landfall. Patients from the Columbia hospitals on Miami Beach—Miami Heart Institute, Miami Beach Community Hospital, and Victoria Hospital—were transported to Deering Hospital in the far south of Dade County instead of evacuating to Columbia's University Hospital in Broward County.

Columbia also informed the staff that they could come with their families and seek shelter at Deering. By the time the storm arrived, Deering's 153 beds were filled to capacity with patients from within its system and beyond, and its meeting rooms and offices were clogged with staff relatives. Tony Degina, then the chief operating officer, recalled, "The last patients we took were four from Mercy Hospital. They got here around six in the evening. Everyone was calm and settled in."

Degina said the hospital had not boarded up the windows in its second-floor patient rooms because it was not considered necessary. Hospital accreditation officials want all patients to have a window so they can stay in contact with the normal cycle of time; and so all hospitals locate patient rooms around the exterior of the building, where they are the most vulnerable to the adverse effects of storms. The accreditation criterion does not, as yet, require that patient windows be equipped with storm shutters. Deering, the shelter selected for three hospitals and their staff, had not even boarded the windows on the ground floor.

Deering's reserve generator was stored in a ground-level bunker and powered by natural gas. One of the maintenance workers produced a box containing a hundred flashlights and offered to distribute them. Degina said he felt there was very little chance they would need the flashlights with the gas-powered generator. Not wanting to cause concern among the patients and staff, he asked that the flashlights remain in storage. "When they finally decided that the storm was going to come ashore right at us, I found that maintenance man and told him that we better not take any chances, that we better distribute the flashlights. As it turned out, that probably saved some of our lives," he said.

Mary Maxine Keesling, a registered nurse, was serving as clinical coordinator in two of Deering's units the night of Andrew. She recalled the succession of events:

> Between 10 and 11 that night we saw the rain increase and the tall palms beginning to bend in the wind. Each time the power flickered it set off all the alarms and buzzers associated with critical-care nursing. I told the nurses on duty to prepare ambu-bags for the ventilator patients. Between 12:30 and 1:00 in the morning, the window-locking devices began to pop open and pound closed. About the time the generator stopped working, the window in the room of a ventilator patient imploded, taking the window and frame apart and sending debris flying into the room. It was time to move our patients to the hall. Those who could sit up were placed in chairs. Others who could not sit up were secured to their beds with sheets.
>
> The staff formed teams of three to work each ventilator patient—one to pump, one to back up the pumper, and one to be a runner. Volunteer pumpers came from all over the hospital.

Degina said he expected the small windows in the patient rooms to withstand the storm. "We moved the patient nearest the window next to the other patient in our two-person rooms and pulled the cloth divider. We figured that if the windows broke, the cloth would at least prevent the patients from being hit by flying glass," he said.

As it turned out, that assumption was hopelessly naive. The windows—all of them—buckled in their aluminum frames and imploded. The rooms became unbearable with the howl of the wind and the deluge of water, so patients who did not need life support were moved to the halls. Fortunately, the doors to patient rooms open inward; the wind blew them closed and sealed them, providing some shelter in the hallway.

Those who needed life support were left in their rooms. At the height of the storm, the window in one intensive-care unit blew in. But the patient was connected to too many machines to be moved easily. While the patient was being disconnected from the machinery, Degina stood in front of the open window, holding a mattress against the frame and shattered glass to slow the blow.

The effort on behalf of the patients on life support shifted gears when the power went out and the emergency generator stopped working. For 12 hours thereafter, volunteers pumped the heart and lung machines that kept the machine-dependent pa-tients alive. They did it calmly and with sufficient care that no patient was lost—and they did it while the hospital was being ripped to pieces.

Sergeant Arthur Gonzalez, a 10-year veteran of the Metro Dade police force, led a contingent of 11 officers who stayed on the streets of South Dade until ordered to take shelter. His group joined the others holed up at Deering. Gonzalez recalled, "Almost as soon as the storm started, our communications failed, except for one frequency. When we heard over the car radios that the worst of the storm was about to hit, we took cover as directed at Deering Hospital."

At the height of the storm, a resident from the neighborhood fought his way to the hospital emergency room only to find the door barricaded with sand bags. Unwilling to allow the man to go without help, the emergency room personnel at Deering opened the doors to let the man in. But as soon as the barricade was removed the doors were ripped open, exposing the emergency room to the full fury of the storm. Dr. Bryan D. Frederick, one of the two emergency room physicians on duty that night, recalled,

The emergency room staff worked together and was prepared to handle just about anything. No patients came between 3:30 a.m. and 6 a.m. However, about 4 a.m., a wild-eyed man appeared at the ER door looking like a drowned rat. We moved the supports from the door and helped him inside. He lived about a half block away. A tree had blown over on his house, and he needed a safe place to stay. Every so often he walked by me, appearing dazed. We never did learn his name.

After we let the man inside, we couldn't reseal the door as tightly. The storm became worse, and soon rainwater and debris were flying around in the ER.

Sergeant Gonzalez recalled,

I heard a commotion that the new emergency room doors on the south side of the hospital were gone. One door was off the hinges. We tried to get it back on and secured it with sandbags. The winds got worse and the other door flopped off its hinges. While some hospital staff members moved supplies and furniture out of the ER, Craig Bauer, Ray Smith, and I went out into the storm to try and pick up the doors and secure them with more sand-bags. While we worked, the wind blew through the emergency room and parts of the ceiling were dropping off.

It was pitch black outside. Debris and rain flew around us, and it was hard to walk erect. I saw a lit flashlight and picked it up. I later learned that the flashlight belonged to Officer Bauer. He had been holding the flashlight when a gust of wind swept him off his feet and sent him tumbling.

The officers found the heavy emergency room doors and carried them back through the hurricane winds. Struggling against the torrent and the wind, the officers wedged the doors in their jambs and packed sandbags against them, effectively sealing off the emergency room so that nothing could enter from the outside. This, of course, made it difficult to get inside the hospital. The officers were forced to stagger between two build-ings through a hail of debris to find their way to an unlocked door. And once they got back inside, they found that the hospital staff had abandoned the emergency room and set up a MASH unit far down the main corridor in the surgical waiting room.

Gonzalez continued,

At about the same time, the hospital's front entrance started flooding, and maintenance crews needed to reinforce the roof latches. Efforts also were made to stop the water running down the heavily traveled stairways.

Patients were moved farther into the center of the patient-care areas as the shaking and rattling of the building's walls grew worse. We could see glass shatter and fly across abandoned rooms into sheet rock which separated from the wall and also flew across the room. Secured doors slammed in their frames. Everyone's feet were wet.

Degina said the water rose to a depth of almost two feet in the hallways, as the storm ripped off the roof at both ends of the building and the rain cascaded down the stairways from the holes in the roof. Occasionally the generator would come on and send pulses of power into the soaked and submerged equipment, shooting sparks and sending smoke into the air. The lights would strobe, then go out.

As the storm raged, a staff engineer volunteered to check the generator and found it was working perfectly. But the rain had invaded the area where the switch was located and shorted it out so that only a random connection was made. Efforts to repair the switch were unsuccessful.

Another engineer figured out a way to stem the rising tide in the hallways, however. Using a sledge hammer, he shattered several of the toilets, creating a series of open drains that carried off the water. The hospital was in shambles by the time the storm broke. But the emergency room continued to treat patients until plans were completed to evacuate Deering's patients to University Hospital in Tamarac.

Columbia's regional executive, Jamie Hopping, the former chief executive officer at Deering, made arrangements with ambulance companies in Broward County. The evacuation was completed with the last patient traveling in a car along with Hopping and two Columbia executives. The patient, elderly and slightly disoriented, thought she was going on a boat ride and complimented Hopping's navigation skills.

Homestead Hospital, associated with South Miami Hospital and located in the area of worst destruction, also took a serious battering. Most of the windows in patient rooms were blown in, driving the 82 patients and care givers into the dark, dank hallways. A portion of the roof was destroyed, and all power was lost.

Despite the damage, Homestead reopened four days after the storm. But 125 of its 350 staff members were left homeless. More than 90 employees quit and left the South Florida area for more placid climes.

Six hospitals—three that had been evacuated and three that remained open during the storm—were closed for a week after the storm because of extensive damage. The hospital at Homestead Air Force Base never reopened.

Another 130 health care facilities were damaged, including 90 ACLFs, two renal dialysis clinics, four mental health sites, and five community health clinics. This total does not include 11 pharmacies that were destroyed and never reopened, along with 1,000 specialty clinics, physicians' offices, and dental clinics.

Incredibly, and more importantly, no patient at a hospital died or endured a significant injury during the storm, and only the emergency rooms at Mercy and Homestead were closed in the impacted area as a result of the storm.

The damage to community health clinics was potentially troublesome because the areas of far South Dade that endured the worst damage were also the poorest and the most reliant on public assistance and public health services. Ironically, the post-Andrew proliferation of volunteer "doc-in-a-box" physicians, field hospitals, and storefront clinics dramatically increased the amount and range of health care services available to the poor of far South Dade. Andrew had the effect of getting medical care to some who had never had it before, and those who had previously paid received care for free.

As Dr. Pedro Greer explained, "There was always a desperate need for an increase in health care services to the poor and migrant workers of South Dade. The storm briefly increased the need for emergency care because of injuries that occurred during the storm-related cleanup. But the storm peeled back the veil and revealed the desperate needs that existed before the storm."

Dr. Greer added, "That area was so underserved we had no idea who was being served and who wasn't. After the storm we discovered an entire tribe of Guatemalan Indians who spoke neither English nor Spanish. They spoke their native Mayan tongue. No one had any idea these people existed."

For many people, the days after Andrew would be described as wind and rain followed by long lines and endless waiting. People waited for food, phones, clothing, water, ice, and mail, among other things. Strings of waiting people curled along roads, through parking lots, in mud and rain, stretching endlessly toward the horizon in place after place.

6

FIRST ASSESSMENT

Anyone who had not visited South Florida before Hurricane
Andrew would have a difficult time appreciating the shock
that came with the dawn. The landscape was totally altered.
Things that could never be seen before through the dense, lush,
tropical foliage now loomed large on the horizon, distorting distances. What trees were left standing were withered and leafless.
No bushes of consequence survived. Every single sign was destroyed, blown away, or damaged. The streets, avenues, driveways, and parking lots were strewn with downed trees, sheet
rock, lumber, and aluminum. Many buildings were only empty
shells.

South Dade is a relatively new area, much of it built in the
past 30 years using technologically advanced materials. Everyone who builds in South Florida is expected to build to withstand
a "typical storm" of 120-mile-per-hour winds and 15 inches of
rain. Andrew was anything but typical. The debate about the
wind puts the sustained velocity anywhere from 140 to 180 miles
per hour. The rain was substantial but insignificant when compared with the wind. When the victims of Andrew and their
would-be rescuers emerged from shelter sometime between seven
and eight in the morning on Monday, August 24, they found
unimaginable damage. It took four months for the toll to be
tallied.

On that hot and soggy day, no one could have known that 92
percent of the power grid in South Florida would need reconstruc-

tion, with 1.4 million, or 84 percent, of FP&L customers in Dade without power—and not likely to get power for more than a week. The darkness was total, with 7,300 street lights down and 21,000 wooden power poles snapped and needing replacement. It would take 34 days before power was restored to 100 percent of the Dade County homes that could accept it. About 24,000 homes were so extensively damaged they were unable to accept power even after it was fully restored.

On Monday morning, when a quick and accurate assessment of the damage and the needs of victims was paramount, 5,300 road signs were down or gone, and only 200 of the region's 2,000 intersections were open. Many emergency personnel who lived in South Dade and were familiar with the area were trapped in their homes or neighborhoods by fallen debris. Volunteer relief workers living in South Dade were likewise trapped or too overwrought by their own situation to leap into action for the general welfare.

Into the void came relief workers and emergency personnel from other parts of the county and the state. The emergency personnel who had experience in the area were disoriented, because they could no longer rely on street signs and landmarks to find their way through South Dade. So it was no surprise that emergency personnel who arrived from Broward County or other areas to the north and west were confounded. Even those who knew their way were confronted with a maze of blocked streets and dead ends.

The destruction was severe below South West 88th Street, and it was difficult to imagine that things could be worse. But imagination was all that many emergency personnel had to rely on for almost two days, because it was impossible to travel into deepest South Dade over land, and the official emergency air force was out of commission.

Like the executives of Columbia Hospital Corporation who had evacuated three hospitals to South Dade, the Dade County emergency officials and Florida Power and Light had put all their eggs in one basket. And that basket—Tamiami Airport in South Dade, near South West 154th Street—was ground zero for Andrew. The police helicopters and the various other agency airplanes and helicopters that had been left at Tamiami for protection were mangled, flipped, or blown away.

With all the airplanes and helicopters destroyed and the roads impassable, the disaster response agencies scrambled to beg or borrow aircraft and get in the air to begin an assessment. A prompt assessment is important for the deployment of emergency resources and for the gathering of information needed for planning the next phase of the relief effort.

In South Florida, as in most communities, the local chapter of the American Red Cross is the designated relief agency in case of disaster. The Dade County chapter of the American Red Cross, like most other Red Cross chapters, spends much of its time on blood drives and fundraising. Nevertheless, it is perpetually short of blood, money, and trained volunteers. The job of recovery falls to the Red Cross and the local governments unless there is a declaration that the local governments are overwhelmed.

Under the federal law known as the Stafford Act, the Federal Emergency Management Agency (FEMA) cannot come into play until the governor of the stricken state asks the president to declare a major disaster. This is defined as a finding on the part of the governor that the scope of the problem is beyond the state's ability to respond.

This rule anticipates that the local agents of the state will be able to assess needs promptly. No such capability existed in South Florida after Andrew, since there were no communications, no open roads, no power, nor any ability to conduct an orderly aerial survey. In addition, the phones that worked were jammed. The main communications link, the Channel 6 tower, had been toppled, and the EOC phones were overloaded and unable to handle either incoming or outgoing calls.

At 10:45 a.m. on Monday, August 24, Florida governor Lawton Chiles declared a state emergency and called in the National Guard, which arrived in some strategic locations by noon. The National Guard units were called in not so much to dig in the debris for survivors or to clear the roads but to counteract the lawlessness that had begun even before the winds subsided, a lawlessness that hindered any other efforts to assist the wounded, locate the dead, or help those in need of food and water.

Mother Nature had issued a credit card to every malefactor in an area filled with crime, poverty, and despair. During most of Monday, looters struck the area south of the city of Kendall with reckless abandon. They pummeled lone police cruisers, forcing the cars to retreat. Emergency personnel driving vehicles that clearly indicated their benevolent intentions were nevertheless shot at so they wouldn't call police who might stop the looting. Likewise, medical emergency vehicles and vehicles carrying public health and public safety personnel were either attacked or stolen. Not the least of the casualties on Day One after Andrew was a truckload of Red Cross supplies that simply disappeared—truck and all—on its way to the city of Homestead.

By the afternoon of the first day, aerial pictures came back from the only helicopters available, those owned by the television stations. The stations, of course, were not doing a systematic survey of the disaster or routes of ingress and egress. They were looking for dramatic images, concentrating on the damage to the coastline and the looting of the posh malls. The images were spectacular. But they bypassed the destruction in Homestead, Naranja, and Florida City.

The staffing shortages at the Red Cross shelters further complicated the rescue effort. The EMTs and paramedics who might otherwise have been available to relieve those on duty during and after the storm were pinned down in the shelters, as thousands of injured and rain-soaked people fled from their demolished homes to the only place they could find help. Since the public health nurses and private duty nurses hired by Dade County failed to show up, the EMT personnel were desperately needed at the shelters.

Michael Weston, who recently had been appointed as director of disaster planning and operation for the Florida Department of Elder Affairs, was pleased with the operation of the local elder affairs unit before the storm. His group was able to notify virtually all of their clients of the need for evacuation, thus catching many of the frail elderly who did not get a notice from the EOC.

Weston was also a coordinator for the Red Cross, stationed at the Dade County EOC bunker during and immediately after the storm. Once the storm had passed, Weston contacted his team of relief workers and prepared to move his 12 trucks full of food and medical supplies into South Dade. The problem he encountered was common to almost everyone else who tried to bring in help from close by. The storm had toppled trees and cluttered the driveways where his trucks had been sheltered.

About midday on Monday, Weston met with Kate Hale, the person in charge of the federal emergency operation in Dade. She told Weston she had a chore for him. The president, George Bush, would be arriving in the afternoon and wanted to drive into the storm-damaged area, Hale told Weston. Weston's job was to supervise the clearing of the roads so that the president could make his prime-time appearance. Weston complained to Hale that the county clean-up crews should be used to clear the way so his trucks could perform their errands of mercy. His priorities were overruled in favor of the presidential tour.

At 6 p.m. President Bush arrived at Miami International Airport and led a motorcade south from the airport along Interstate 95 to a partially cleared U.S. 1, then on to a partially cleared Old Cutler Road, a tree-lined lane through one of Miami's most affluent areas. Bush went as far as the road had been cleared—to Cutler Ridge, near property developed by one of his sons, where he posed by a damaged tree. The visit took no more than two hours, including a nationally televised speech. In three hours Bush was back in the air, and South Florida was designated a federal disaster area.

The seriousness of the disaster was self-evident to its isolated victims. But its full scope was not known for a week. No one had ever seen such widespread devastation from such a compact storm. Each place a survey team arrived appeared to be the site of the worst possible devastation. Hours later, a few miles further south or west, a new ground zero would be declared. This assessment shortfall has been identified as the greatest flaw in the short-term recovery effort that followed Andrew.

If President Bush's party had tried to drive a few miles farther south along U.S. 1, the entire nation would have known what remained a mystery for two more days: the total destruction of two small towns and a major air force base. But no one was available to do a quick and efficient needs assessment, and as federal relief efforts are currently organized, help is available only if the disaster is official and only if needs are precisely specified.

Dexter Peach, the assistant comptroller general of the United States, described the problem:

> The Federal Response Plan developed by FEMA after Hurricane Hugo does not have a support function that addresses the

performance of damage and needs assessments, even though the plan itself recognizes that the magnitude of damage to structures and lifelines will rapidly overwhelm the capacity of state and local government to assess the disaster and respond effectively to basic and emergency needs. In practice, their request for federal assistance must specify the type, amount, and location of the needed services. State and local governments were unable to do this because of the overwhelming nature of Hurricane Andrew, causing delays in services.

Local officials, who in many cases were victims of the storm, knew they were unable to meet their citizens' needs for life-sustaining services. However, they were having trouble communicating with one another and with the state and were unable to request specific assistance.

FEMA's director told us that FEMA is limited by the Stafford Act to responding only to state requests for assistance. [Therefore] FEMA could not help the state unless it asked for assistance and specified how much it needed.

Not everyone holds this interpretation of the Stafford Act, however. Peach and his group interpret the law to mean that once the president declares a national disaster, FEMA "has the authority to conduct it own damage and needs assessment and then recommend to the state specific amounts of assistance that should be requested."

The debate over assessment criteria and timing is an important lesson for health care providers in disaster-prone areas. Recommendations for revision of the law include provisions for damage and needs assessment by federal agencies. But the assessment cannot begin until a day after the storm and cannot be completed until two days after the storm. That means an organized federal response would not be likely until three days after the storm has passed, leaving medical facilities only one option: prepare to survive with no help for at least three days after the storm.

Ironically, U.S. intelligence satellites could have provided real-time information about the damage caused by Andrew. Military reconnaissance aircraft could have provided valuable, detailed photographs of the entire region within a day and detailed surveillance information that could have been processed within hours.

According to Florida EOC director Frank Koutnik, the State of Florida never conducted a needs assessment or a damage assessment after Hurricane Andrew. He said that after the presidential declaration of a disaster area was made, the state argued that there was no need for a formal assessment. According to Koutnik, the state left it up to Dade County to conduct a needs assessment, which would provide the specifics required under the Stafford Act. Dade said it could not do the assessment and insisted the state take action. As Koutnik recalled,

> I was in the discussion over damage assessment and needs assessment with Phil May, the regional director, and we twisted Phil's arm and said, "Why do we need to waste time and go do a damage assessment?" He wanted to go do a preliminary damage assessment. Our logic was that we already had the presidential declaration, so why did we need it? Who gives a hoot how many buildings have shingles missing when you are trying to help people? Our problem was that we only had plans to do a damage assessment and not a needs assessment. We looked to the county and the county looked back to us. It was a foreign concept to us.
>
> You heard it was not until August 29 that the state hit the street. But the truth of the matter is that the state never hit the street. We learned that lesson big time. We are going to need rapid response teams whose only job is to get into the county and then come back with the information. We are going to need star-wars technology with fly-overs and satellite tie-ins looking at a damaged area, tied in with tax assessors' records. This will be tied in to a computer, which will spit out a report that will be our damage assessment. And that report will drive our needs assessment.

Even with the innovations planned for Florida, the system will remain untested until the next major storm. Not all states will follow Florida's lead in expediting damage assessment. Nor is it certain that the computer will anticipate the complex needs of those affected facilities and individuals in the health care delivery system.

So it makes sense for health care facilities and agencies to establish a procedure that assures that they can deliver adequate emergency health care and provide for basic public health needs for at least 72 hours after a disaster—without any assistance from any organized outside entity. Each individual organization must develop a three-day survival plan using its own resources in isolation or in cooperation with the political subdivision it serves, counting on no outside help, utilities, or reinforcements. Such a plan must include provisions for medical supplies, gases, dressings, food, water for drinking, water for cleaning, water for flushing toilets, fuel and batteries, electrical lights powered by batteries and generators, communications equipment, back-up personnel, ventilation, transportation, security, nonautomated record keeping, fundamental film processing, and a clear policy on admissions and transfers.

Much has been learned from Hurricane Andrew. But it must be pointed out that much was learned from Hurricane Hugo—then forgotten. Since past is prelude, what actually happened within the health care system in the days after Andrew is worth reviewing.

Fatigue is the inevitable companion of natural disaster. The face of Kate Hale, Dade County emergency operations manager, reflects the pressure of long days, great stress, and inadequate support when it was most needed. Thousands of others, contributing in large ways and small, felt as she did, weary but determined to serve the victims of Hurricane Andrew.

7

DAY ONE: CONFRONTING CHAOS

Almost everyone who was on the scene in far South Dade during the first week following Hurricane Andrew has difficulty remembering what happened and when it happened. Those first few days are a blur, filled with desperate efforts to reinvent order, stay dry, fight mosquitoes, get something to eat and drink, and find time to sleep. The first day after the storm is characterized as one in which efforts to reestablish communications and learn the dimensions of the disaster were paramount and generally unsuccessful. It was, for the most part, a day of digging out, clearing short paths, and reconnecting. Monday is recalled as a resolution of Sunday. Tuesday is the fulfillment of Monday's frustrations. Wednesday is when things seemed to begin happening. Thursday is about the time everyone realized they were in it for the long haul. Beyond that, it is difficult for the participants to isolate specific events to the day they actually occurred.

Dade County has 26 municipalities, each of which was theoretically entitled to send a representative to the primary Dade EOC. But the primary Dade EOC had no room for representatives from all the cities during or after the storm, so the county allowed only 6 cities to be present, representing all 26.

Jim Hampton, the city manager of the City of South Miami, was not one of the representatives. His experience provides a way to understand the communication dilemma faced by other cities that suffered even greater destruction. Hampton could not get in touch with any officials in Dade County until Friday of the first week; nor was he contacted or informed officially of any recovery plan. The lack of communication was disturbing to him, since his city suffered relatively little damage, many phones continued in operation, and it straddles the main routes to far South Dade, making it strategically important.

For the first four days, as he waited for instructions, convoys of trucks and cadres of medical volunteers would show up at the South Miami city hall, wondering where the fight for survival was being waged. Many confused the City of South Miami with the area generally described as South Dade. Hampton had no way of providing official directions, so he simply sent them south and busied himself with his city's concerns.

Most of the South Dade area is unincorporated and therefore the exclusive responsibility of the Metropolitan Dade County government. Homestead and Florida City were the only municipalities in the area of severe destruction. Under the current system, with its hierarchies of relief, the cities must beg the counties for help, the counties must beg the state, and the state must beg the federal government. If you don't ask, no help can be expected. And asking was a real problem after Hurricane Andrew.

Since the Dade County EOC building was built to withstand devastation from a nuclear attack, its walls are shielded, making it impossible to use a cellular phone or radio from inside the building. With its phone system crippled by poor planning and the massive demand, with the Dade County police command in South Dade limited to only one line, with all power out in the area, with official aircraft destroyed at Tamiami Airport, the Dade County EOC had no way to initiate communications with Homestead or Florida City those first few days, except to travel through the heart of the destruction or hope for a lucky phone connection.

Homestead City Manager Alex Muxo, his home destroyed and his city in shambles, finally made contact with the EOC at 2:05 p.m. on Monday—Day One. His message: "Ninety percent wiped out. Twenty to thirty thousand homeless. Won't have water until next week. Biggest need is port-o-lets."

Muxo's community was not the only place suffering a toilet crisis. Back at the Dade EOC, one of the emergency generators failed soon after the storm, plunging the bunker into temporary chaos and reducing the water pressure for the bunker's limited lavatory facilities. The 150 crisis planners, already in their 24th consecutive hour of work, found themselves working in a room fouled by clogged toilets that would not flush. Someone finally decided to issue a garbage can of water with every bowel movement to prime the toilets.

At the Dade EOC, Day One was spent patching together failed systems, scrambling for information, arguing with visiting state officials, and preparing for a presidential visit. At the Florida State EOC in Tallahassee, the staff was alternately attempting to learn what had happened 800 miles away and what was happening in Gov. Lawton Chiles's conference room, where the politicians had assembled and usurped the role of the professional planners. Much of the day was spent trying, unsuccessfully, to get through on the telephone to the Dade EOC.

According to Mike Williams, state coordinator of emergency management services (EMS), the state set up a separate state EOC solely for health services. He called it "probably the smartest thing we ever did."

He said, "After the storm passed, our number-one problem was communications. There was none between Tallahassee and Dade County, absolutely none. There was one line going into the Dade EOC. Needless to say, that puppy was jammed beyond control. So we did not know what the situation was down there."

Governor Chiles had flown to Miami early in the day on Day One. When it was clear no airplanes were available to do an assessment, he asked the state EOC to contact other agencies. The first call went out to the Civil Air Patrol, which is tasked in the state emergency plan with conducting an aerial assessment. The patrol refused, citing bad weather. "They laughed uncontrollably and said there is no way," Williams recalled.

Next, the state asked the U.S. Air Force for satellite or military fly-overs. But the military said the cloud cover was too dense. Finally, Chiles sent his brand new state airplane to carry emergency personnel and to use for an aerial survey.

"[One of] the first . . . agencies they wanted down there [was] the Department of Environmental Regulation, which controls the removal of debris, and they also had a key role in water and porta-potties. That is the number-one thing in a situation like this. Get the water, get the porta-potties, and you can get through everything else," Williams said.

At the Red Cross shelters in South Dade, the normal pattern following a natural disaster was reversed. Instead of the typical reduction in occupancy once a storm passes, the numbers increased dramatically. Those families whose houses had been destroyed around them fled to the already crowded hurricane shelters. They had nowhere else to go. But the shelters were not designed to house refugees after a storm, and they were already running out of water and food.

When those families who had weathered the storm in the shelters heard about the devastation, they were anxious to learn the fate of their homes, pets, and valuables. Rather than requiring them to stay in the shelters for a few days, thereby reducing the complexity of providing for public health and safety, the shelter managers were glad to release some of their burden. And, because supplies were short, no effort was made to send the families home with the food, water, and protective gear that most of them would immediately need. The flow of families returning to their destroyed homes in South Dade created an immediate law enforcement problem.

Even before the winds had subsided, thousands of people swarmed over the area of devastation, looting stores and homes. While it would have been wiser, in retrospect, to restrict access to the damaged area, it was impossible to separate the looters from the homeowners attempting to salvage some personal treasure. And it was impossible to separate the gawkers from those who needed to get home or wanted to aid their stricken families.

"After Hugo we felt that we were fully prepared for everything," said Ed Neafsey, assistant fire chief for operations. "Nothing but nothing could have prepared us for the crises caused by Andrew." He described the situation:

> As the winds subsided we were faced with over 250 priority calls. We had screened out over 1,500 nonpriority calls. We had 600 square miles of devastated area, damaged fire stations and apparatus, little to no communication from command to field units. We found ourselves both the rescuer and the victim. We know now that every hurricane plan must address the psychological stress the loss of homes puts on your fire fighters and command staff.
>
> As we moved into the response mode, things kept getting worse. Our department logged 1,250 calls. Our normal average

for the day was 350. And for every call that we logged, our staff told us that they handled at least three calls from people who would simply wave them down. Our best guess is that we handled 3,000. In most areas it took us an hour to go a mile with the debris in the way and the tremendous problem we had with flat tires. What we had was a 625-square-mile triage area, and the nearest operating medical facility over 25 miles away. We were faced with hundreds of people who needed emergency care with no place to take them. In addition, there were thousands who needed the basic necessities of life—simply food, water, and shelter. And I am here to tell you that for the first 24 to 48 hours, the EMT and fire services are going to be the ones to provide those things. The resources they put in place prior to the storm are going to be all you have to work with. No matter how effective the system is, it is not going to get you support for at least that length of time. Simply because the fire and rescue units are in the neighborhoods, people are going to look to them.

Neafsey said the region was divided into grids, and 900 fire fighters and rescue specialists were each given a map of their assigned area, a radio, and a promise of a hot meal at the end of the day. The teams went door to door asking if anyone was missing. They used dogs to search crumpled buildings, looking for the dead. The death toll attributed directly to the storm was 15.

The official fire department incident log shows the progression of various types of injuries and other emergencies encountered during the first few days. On Day One, the first two cases were cardiac, the next a childbirth. Many of the earliest calls were for individuals having trouble breathing. The maternity calls continued all day long. By midday, individuals who had lost their medication began to experience seizures, and the number of slip and fall injuries increased as people attempted to climb through debris. As night approached, the number of mugging victims increased, as did the number of auto accidents. And, in one bizarre hour, apparently after the shock of the storm had worn off and desperation set in, there were three suicide attempts.

Since the two $5-million helicopters belonging to the fire department's air rescue unit were destroyed, there was no capacity for air rescue, however serious the injury, for 32 hours after the storm. The fire department's Hurricane Andrew After Action Report describes the situation on Day One:

The number of serious injuries directly related to Andrew was low. However, as people began to clean up debris, the number of injuries rose quickly. This, along with the backlog of calls, placed a great strain on the department, especially since there were no medical facilities available. Fire/rescue units soon found that all the primary and secondary medical care facilities in South Dade County were severely damaged and unable to accept any patients. This added to the strain on the pre-hospital emergency care system, since all patients in need of definitive care had to be transported to other hospitals. Baptist Hospital of Miami, on S.W. 88 Street, over an hour away under the circumstances, was the closest. In addition, patients already in the affected hospitals had to be moved to other facilities.

As a result, the Miami Dade Fire Department requested that Randle and Medi-Car ambulance companies make available their units for the transport of fire/rescue patients. Their participation allowed most fire/rescue units to stay in the affected zones to provide the much-needed care.

With no medical facilities south of Kendall Drive, MDFD took the initiative to begin organizing and staffing field hospitals. The first one was located in the new government center building.

Captain Ellery Gray, with the National Disaster Medical System (NDMS), a branch of the U.S. Public Health Service, had been pre-staged in the Dade County EOC. Captain Gray facilitated the quick deployment and establishment of two field hospitals requested by MDFD. These free-standing facilities are each staffed by a Disaster Medical Assistance Team. They consist of 36 medical personnel and are capable of providing sophisticated emergency medical care in an austere setting. Their first field hospital relieved the first aid facility started by MDFD in the new South Dade government center.

By design the field hospitals are almost totally self-sufficient. However, in order for them to function efficiently, close coordination with the local EMS system is necessary. MDFD personnel were assigned to act as liaison officers in coordinating transportation of patients to and from the field hospitals.

The report also pointed out another problem:

Damage to fire stations' overhead doors, coupled with the number of people left homeless and without food and water, created a security problem as they loitered around the local fire stations.

The department could not access the proper mechanism to authorize personnel, such as National Guard, Metro-Dade Police Department, or Florida Highway Patrol, to provide permanent security for the fire stations and their resources and supplies. As a result, a considerable amount of equipment was reported missing.

When Governor Chiles called in the National Guard on Monday morning, the troops were responding to a martial law situation and had no time for other, more humanitarian goals. Looters were so prevalent and brazen that they attacked and fired upon any vehicle entering the area that looked official for fear the occupants would call in the beleaguered police to end the plunder. Chaos reigned. The situation was particularly bad in Homestead, which was left to fend for itself because of its municipal status. The situation was even more desperate in Florida City, the fifth-poorest city in America, which was both destroyed and bankrupted by the storm.

The health care system was equally devastated. The hospital at Homestead Air Force Base was destroyed. Another facility, Homestead Hospital, which had recently merged with South Miami Hospital, was virtually destroyed. It continued to operate a crisis facility without power or a roof until it was compelled to relocate its patients and close. Deering Hospital was severely damaged and forced to close after a day in which workers kept respirator patients alive manually while treating the walking wounded. It had neither power nor water. The roof had been peeled back, all the windows blown in. The emergency room had been gutted.

Baptist Hospital's emergency room, which typically saw fewer than 100 patients on a busy, full-moon Friday night, was inundated with more than 600 walk-ins. Though damaged by the storm and without water, Baptist stayed open. Likewise, South Miami Hospital saw its emergency patient caseload quadruple the first day and swell for weeks thereafter.

Many of the special-needs patients in South Dade found themselves with no place to go. More than 1,000 beds in nursing homes that provided skilled care and 533 beds in adult congregate living facilities ceased to exist.

Only one medical facility in far South Dade survived the hurricane relatively unscathed. The Suburban Medical Center, just off U.S. 1 in Perrine, in the epicenter of destruction, is a two-story structure designed to support several more floors. The facility included 3 operating rooms and an endoscopy room, a 5-bed recovery room, and 18 patient rooms with 26 beds.

Jules Gary Minkes, a doctor of osteopathy and director of Suburban, told the magazine *The DO* that the storm did more than $500,000 damage to his facility, particularly in the library and records room and in the surgical center, where water damaged some linens and surgical instruments. Minkes had built the facility to meet the requirements for the small neighborhood medical centers that were advocated during the 1970s. But under existing laws, Suburban was classified as a clinic and could not keep patients overnight. For several years Minkes had attempted to secure accreditation as a hospital. But resistance from the competing hospitals in the area and the glut of hospital rooms worked against him.

On Day One after Andrew, it seemed that fate had placed Suburban Medical Center in exactly the right place at the right time. But the facility and its substantial resources were totally ignored.

As night approached that first day, the newly homeless awaited official word that help was on the way. They packed their valuables, built shelters, and tried to rig a way to store and chill their remaining food supplies. With no power for miles in every direction and brazen looters on the prowl, it was the darkest and most dangerous night in the history of South Florida. Yet there was a sense of elation among the survivors, a giddiness that resulted from two days with little sleep, residual adrenaline, and the pure power of having survived a life-threatening situation.

In Homestead and Florida City, according to one published study, one-third of the families who remained at home during the storm spent the peak hours of the blow with nothing more than a mattress between them and the killer winds. Many of them would spend the next week with even less in the way of assistance or protection.

Mute testimony to the destructive power of a hurricane is reflected at a single homesite in South Dade. Where lush foliage, a landscaped yard, and a bright and cheerful home once existed, there remained only a skeleton of yesterday. Denuded and bent trees, a battered house, debris and clutter from unknown sources were all that was left to contemplate.

8

DAY TWO:
AD HOC AD INFINITUM

The Dade County EOC had been quick to ask for help. In fact, the EOC had contacted the White House and had asked for a presidential declaration of emergency on Sunday night, several hours before the storm arrived. And the EOC had called for special emergency medical help from federal Disaster Medical Assistance Teams (DMAT) long before the winds had subsided, according to hurricane coordinator Michele Baker.

The federal DMAT team from the Southeast Region assembled at Eglin Air Force Base in the Florida Panhandle the morning of Day Two. The team consisted of 50 civilian and military men and women—physicians, nurses, paramedics, emergency medical technicians, radio operators, and fire fighters—who had been trained specifically to fly into disaster areas and provide short-term emergency medical care. They had been to summer camp to train for the mission. But Andrew was their first real test.

The DMAT team was required to sign release forms to exonerate the federal government from liability before they could fly on the giant C-130 aircraft that had been provided for the trip from the Panhandle to South Florida. As they waited, several vans full of donated medicine and supplies arrived on the tarmac. Eager to get on with the mission and unfamiliar with the huge aircraft, the DMAT team began packing the gray and green bay with the donated stores, pleased that they would be so well supplied. As the last of it was crammed inside and the engines started, the DMAT team was shocked to see that most of their personal belongings and some of the medical gear were still lying on the runway, about to be left behind. "The C-130s look bigger than they are," one team member noted. Rather than take off for Miami, the plane was shut down, unpacked, and repacked with greater attention to priorities.

As the big plane winged toward Opa Locka Airport, a crew of volunteers who had driven across the state from Lee County on the west coast of Florida arrived at Florida City. They had followed the back roads through the Everglades to reach the east coast, and serendipity placed them at Florida City.

The volunteers from Lee County found chaos among the survivors in Florida City. The city had no emergency management plan. Its 17 police officers were immobilized because their building and the city's five patrol cars had been destroyed. The entire infrastructure had dissolved in the storm and the rains that followed. There was no power and there were no phones or radio communication.

The only building left standing was the water tower. The city of 15,000, most of whom were indigent, unemployed, or seasonal workers, suffered 80 percent destruction of its tax base. Housing, which had consisted primarily of mobile homes or public apartments, was, for the most part, destroyed. The city had an annual budget of only $4 million, no savings, no credit, and no idea what to do even when, on the second day, volunteers showed up to drop off supplies. There was no place—official or unofficial—where food, medicine, or clothing could be stored out of the weather. As supplies arrived they were stacked in open lots, only to be soaked and rendered useless by the rainstorms that pelted the survivors every afternoon. Recognizing the desperateness of the situation, the Lee County volunteers decided to make their stand among the survivors of Florida City. They set up a tent hospital, complete with a communications bus and two ambulances.

From Kendall and Homestead, hundreds of residents rushed north to try to get ice from the Royal Palm Ice factories in Dade and Broward counties. In the afternoon, before the rains, the temperature rose to 93 degrees, and people wanted to preserve the food in their refrigerators—food that they hoped would keep them going until power was returned, the stores reopened, or help arrived with new food.

Meanwhile, the Metro Dade Water and Sewer Department surveyed its devastated system and declared a water emergency. Backup pumps and generators did not work as promised, and the possibility of a public health crisis affecting more than a million citizens without potable water reared its rancid head.

Florida Power and Light estimated 779,500 customers in Dade County and 132,000 in Broward County were without power. It promised to restore power to all of Palm Beach, Broward, and Collier counties by August 27. But the delivery system that served South Dade would have to be rebuilt, and the FP&L planners quietly agreed that it could be months before the last home was connected.

Across the region, the looting that had begun as pure plunder became more an act of desperation. A woman and her three children were caught looting a drug store in front of security guards and reporters. "God forgive me, but my children don't have anything. My house is destroyed. I don't have money. I'm living in my car," she said.

In Florida City several on-duty police officers hijacked a water truck headed to Homestead and diverted it to parched constituents. At 3 p.m., 29 hours after they had arrived to protect the Cutler Ridge Mall, near the epicenter of the storm, the National Guard arrived in Florida City.

At 4:30 p.m. Charles F. Pierce, president of the Florida Hospital Association, sent a fax transmission to the chief operating officers of the member hospitals:

> South Florida hospitals need supplies and personnel. Early information from South Florida indicates many hospitals are struggling to maintain services in the face of power outages and lack of personnel and supplies such as food and water. Many roads are impassable, making transfers of patients difficult. The homes of many hospital employees have been damaged, and they and their families are staying at their hospitals. At least two hospitals in the path of Hurricane Andrew—SMH Homestead and Deering Hospital—are reported closed due to severe damage. When the storm hit Monday morning, the hospitals were caring for many patients evacuated from other hospitals on Sunday. Hospitals able to provide assistance should call a special HRS hot line Aug. 24–25 at 904/488-0390. Further information will be available in the news media.

Pierce advised the members, "The FHA is in touch with HCFA and the Medicare fiscal intermediary concerning transferring patients between hospitals."

The South Florida Hospital Association began its damage assessment on Monday and reported on Tuesday the status of 13 hospitals affected by the storm:

[Baptist Hospital] served as receiving hospital for evacuated patients from Miami Beach/Coral Gables; having difficulty getting physicians.

[Deering] served as receiving hospital for evacuated patients from Miami Beach area; windows imploded, water everywhere; patients being evacuated; hospital totally closed; suppliers having difficulty getting to hospitals; linens in short supply; patients going to Kendall, Miami Beach, and Victoria—transportation a problem.

[Kendall] served as a receiving hospital for evacuated patients from Miami Beach; no major damage; taking patients from Deering; not accepting other patients unless it's an emergency.

[Cedars of Lebanon] served as a receiving hospital for evacuated hospitals; some windows out, trees down; ER patients still being admitted but not electives; minor problems experienced.

[North Shore] served as receiving hospital for evacuated patients from Miami Beach/Coral Gables.

[Jackson Memorial] served as receiving hospital for evacuated patients from Miami Beach/Coral Gables; initiated call for pregnant women in last three weeks of pregnancy to stay at JMH; suffered some damage, water/windows out.

[Miami Beach] evacuated on Sunday; now taking patients from Deering; holding its own, no real damage.

[Victoria] closed Sunday, reopened Monday; taking patients from Deering; CEO's house pretty well gone; needs nursing and allied health personnel; hospital structural integrity appears OK.

[Memorial] structural integrity great, only two windows out; beds available at both locations for patients in following areas: med/surg, ICU, ped ICU and antepartum. Hospitals are fully staffed, expect to be back to normal operations by this afternoon.

[Golden Glades] very minor damage; staying tight with 78 patients; concerned that BFI not responding to waste disposal calls.

[South Miami] structural damage pretty bad, power gone, water damage; needs nursing staff support; SMH Homestead a disaster—hit very badly—will need to be totally rebuilt; looking to evacuate Homestead; patients that are at South Miami need nurses in following areas: OB, LD, med/surg, ER; have been told major arteries [streets] are open/passable—asking for any nursing support at all; at full occupancy.

[Coral Gables] possibly lost their parking garage.

[Westchester] some serious roof damage, fair amount of water damage, power and water problems under control; needs to find fuel, any thoughts? Needs nursing staff—working off skeleton crew—taking emergency patients only.

[Bon Secours, a nursing home in the northern end of the county] did not evacuate; limited structural damage; roof, windows out; on emergency power; no water—needs City of North Miami to give special consideration to get water back on; staffing OK, but everyone is tired.

Jo Anne Cox, an executive with Florida Health Care Associates, was the person who took charge of the recovery operations for the region's nursing homes. She said that the evacuation of the special-needs individuals went reasonably well, although problems mounted rapidly after the storm.

Saint Anne's Nursing Center and Residence was one of nine nursing home facilities destroyed by the storm. But it had not been evacuated because it was not considered at risk. Instead St. Anne's was used as a shelter for its own residents and dozens of other special-needs individuals. Those who sought refuge at St. Anne's survived the traumatic night, but the situation was difficult after the storm.

The region's nursing homes had no plan for recovery, Cox said. On Tuesday, Day Two, she began receiving calls with offers of donations from all over the nation. One hospital in Jacksonville was sending down a truck full of supplies. But Cox, like Hampton in the City of South Miami, had no idea where to tell them to go. Like Hampton, she attempted to call the Dade EOC but could not get through.

She and Larry Mankoff, another nursing home administrator, established their own ad hoc emergency management program for the special-needs people who had been evacuated from South Dade to facilities in other areas. "There was no plan. It just materialized," she recalled. Mankoff established a staging point and distribution center at Miami Gardens Care Center in North

Dade and in the next few days accepted and redistributed more than half a million pounds of supplies, including gasoline.

Meanwhile, the Disaster Medical Assistance Team arrived at Cutler Ridge from Eglin Air Force Base. It set up a temporary field hospital in the median of the road, adjacent to the blown-out Cutler Ridge government center, opposite the Cutler Ridge Mall. The DMAT unit had been established three years earlier. "We all had trained for the contingency of Andrew. Andrew was our first deployment into the field, so a lot of training was put to the test," recalled team member and trauma specialist Dr. Charles Neal.

The DMAT team wore uniforms that included T shirts of varying colors to indicate whether the team member's function was administrative, clerical, or medical. "We flew to Opa Locka, then hopped to Cutler Ridge, where we set up our first tent that night opposite the government center. We called it the DMAT Hilton," Neal said. "There was no potable water, although water was available from a nearby fire hydrant, where two showers were erected using wooden boxes, served by fire hoses."

The DMAT team carried its own food and water for seven days so it could be totally self-supporting. It did not carry food and water to share, however. (Federal DMAT teams are supposed to come in for five to seven days, and then team members rotate back to their regular jobs.) A second DMAT team arrived later in the day and was sent to Homestead, where it set up a field hospital at a senior citizens center.

Neal described the situation he encountered:

> Nothing prepared me for what I was getting into. The denuded trees, the destruction, the smell of death and kerosene, gave a war zone feeling. The people were all very well shell-shocked. Our food supply was questionable. There were always some nice little old ladies who were making sandwiches out of some meat they did not want to throw away when their refrigerator went bad, and they were constantly bringing food to us. But because there were only two physicians in the team, if one of us came down with dysentery, our team efficiency would go down, so I restricted my diet to meals ready to eat [MREs].

When the army finally arrived, at the end of the first week, the DMAT crew found themselves billeted for sleeping within 30 yards of the landing and refueling area of the helicopters being used to fly in supplies. "You can't talk. You can't even open your eyes when one of them is taking off or landing," according to Neal.

After the first week, the DMAT field hospital was moved to a former bank and divided into three color-coded zones. The green area, for the walking wounded, was where tetanus shots were administered and simple puncture wounds were treated. Bank teller windows were converted into three suturing bays that were in operation nonstop for the first few days. The yellow area was for the more serious trauma patients, and the red section was the cardiac section.

"We were seeing 500 patients a day. Also we had to improvise to build everything we needed from scratch. We saw a lot of traumatic injuries that resulted from debris removal and were usually cuts and scrapes and puncture wounds," Neal recalled.

By the end of the second day, free-lance volunteer medical teams began arriving in vans and mobile homes. They became known as the "doc-in-a box" medical corps. Neal told of problems related to validating medical licenses:

> We had a lot of people who showed up at our doors with a stethoscope around their necks who said, "Hey, I am a doctor or nurse and I want to help." And it turned out that many of them were not. It was kind of a sick thing, but it repeated itself time and time again. So we established a policy that DMAT team members had ultimate control of our facility, and that everything that we said went. It was law, no questions asked, either our way or the highway. Then and only then would we accept volunteers.

Neal said they also patrolled the area they were serving to locate rival bands of doctors and make sure they were appropriately credentialed. Along the way they found a group of medical residents working out of a van Neal said was stolen. "We closed them down," he said.

With its paramilitary training, the DMAT team tolerated little in terms of interference with its mission. But it wasn't without heart. "We took care of everybody who had a problem," Neal recalled. "This little kid drove up with his dad. He was in the back of a pickup truck with his dog. The dog had been hit with debris and his ear had almost been cut off. I am not a vet, nor am

I licensed to do veterinary work. But what was I going to tell this kid who was crying there, holding his dog? So we sewed up the dog's ear and put him on some antibiotics."

Elaine Gorman works for the Health Care Trauma District of the Upper Keys, transporting seriously injured patients to Jackson Memorial Hospital in Dade County. When it was predicted that the Upper Keys would be hit by Andrew and should be evacuated, she and other members of her unit of Monroe County employees evacuated their ambulances up Route 27 to Okeechobee, Florida.

Meanwhile, Monroe County sent its special-needs patients to the designated Monroe County hurricane shelter at the Florida International University (FIU) campus in southwest Dade County, along with a contingent of EMT personnel and paramedics to assist in their care.

After the storm had passed, the trauma district's two ambulances and trauma vehicle made their way back to Monroe County through the rubble, arriving around noon on Monday. On the way back, the unit was contacted by a Monroe County sheriff's deputy and dispatched to FIU to pick up Monroe patients from the shelter and transport them back home. In the meantime, the Key Largo volunteer fire department had begun setting up an ad hoc command post in a McDonalds restaurant in Florida City.

By the morning of the second day, various emergency operations centers had been set up, each trying to hold its own ground and connect with the others. Tallahassee had two or three EOCs, depending on one's point of view. The official state EOC remained in operation but out of the decision-making loop, because Governor Chiles had taken charge. He assigned Carol Browner, then head of the state's Department of Environmental Regulation, Tom Herndon, his chief of staff, and state EMS coordinator Mike Williams to South Dade to conduct a needs assessment and organize the effort. Williams, meanwhile, had set up his own EOC for health-related issues at his Tallahassee office to coordinate all the medical, paramedical, nursing, public health, and EMS personnel and relief efforts.

Dade County's EOC continued in operation in West Dade. But a second EOC was already springing up at the government center in Cutler Ridge as the National Guard, local police, and the DMAT team huddled together, beyond the reach of normal communications.

Another ad hoc EOC was established in Homestead among city officials, personnel from the second DMAT team field hospital, and the National Guard. Yet another was established by the volunteers from Lee County in Florida City. The nursing home community established an EOC in northern Dade County to help feed and house their displaced constituents. And according to the MDFD After Action Report, there was a "doc-in-the-box" on almost every corner in the area north of Florida City. The MDFD report stated:

> Because South Miami/Homestead Hospital and Deering Hospital, the two major facilities serving south Dade County, and two large [public] health clinics were closed due to storm damage, and almost all physicians' offices and primary care clinics in the devastated area were completely destroyed, basic first aid and primary health care services were also provided by a large contingent of volunteer health care personnel. Many private organizations or groups set up temporary "first aid stations" or "clinics." They operated out of recreational vehicles, vans, and tents in the devastated areas. At times there was almost one clinic per each square mile of populated land. Some of these clinics provided community outreach. Health professionals either drove or walked door-to-door to provide the medical assessments and care to the homebound, infirm, or those who feared leaving their homes.
>
> While poorly organized from a systems perspective, these clinics fulfilled an immediate need and reduced the number of minor injuries treated by fire/rescue, hospital emergency rooms, and field hospitals. Unfortunately, the numerous clinics weren't integrated into the EMS system because they could not or would not access MDFD Medical Communications or the 911 system; therefore the presence of most of the clinics was unknown to MDFD. As phone service was restored (two weeks into the process) and access became more immediate through the 911 system, MDFD was, for the most part, able to integrate this resource into the system.

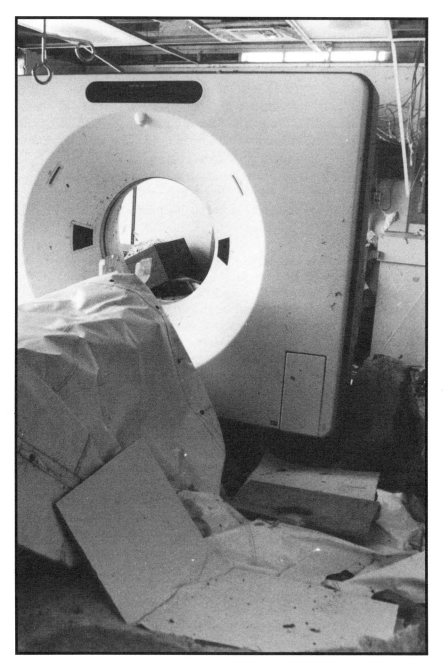

A CAT scanner lies twisted and broken beyond repair at Deering Hospital. Damage done to the building and facilities was frightening, but overcome by the courage of the staff and patients in the face of the storm. Five critically ill patients on respirators and 149 others were carried down stairways and shuttled to other hospitals in ambulances, buses, and back seats.

DAYS THREE AND FOUR: JOINING HANDS, HELPING HANDS

By Wednesday it was clear to all the participants in the rescue and recovery effort that the rescue was virtually over, but the recovery was taking too long to get underway. The storm had caused far fewer deaths and serious injuries than anyone would have expected by viewing the damage. A large number of fire fighters and rescue workers had marched into Dade County prepared to pay back the famous South Florida fire fighters who had, in previous years, flown all over the world sharing their special skills in urban search and rescue. Unfortunately, after the second day, the outsiders were neither needed nor had anyone made arrangements to accommodate them.

One entire unit from Jacksonville drove through the night to Miami. By the time they arrived there was little to do. Fortunately, they had brought their own food and sleeping gear, so they were not, like hundreds of others, an expensive burden on the local fire fighters. They drove around for a couple of days shooting videos of each other amidst the devastation, and then went home.

The crush of fire fighter volunteers was similar to the crush of volunteers from the medical profession. Many more showed up than were actually needed to treat hurricane-related injuries. The fire fighters quickly set up a system to deflect the tide of unneeded help with some element of tact. The medical profession did not.

By the fourth day, the fire fighters had secured the assistance of the fire department in St. Petersburg, Florida, to act as the official agency in charge of logistics, resupply, and personnel under the long-standing tradition of fire fighters' mutual aid agreements. Like the power companies, the fire fighters have formal and informal mutual aid agreements, whereby departments from as far as 1,000 miles away assemble trained volunteers to travel to crisis areas to assist if needed or to back up the local forces and fill in when the locals need a break. These people have standardized training and universally recognized certification. They are willing to submit to a unified command and are guaranteed compensation from their local jurisdictions.

The federally sponsored DMAT teams are similar in many ways to their fire fighter counterparts. They are streamlined, self-contained, paramilitary in organization, and ready to travel to areas that have experienced great devastation, trauma, and loss of life.

After Day One, what South Florida needed was an army of primary care physicians, general practitioners, public health nurses, and pediatricians armed with a barrel of tetanus inoculations and accompanied by a phalanx of psychologists. What it got instead were hundreds of both skilled and inept medical personnel who were convinced there was a trauma crisis, there were hordes in need of saving, and there was enough glory to go around.

To take care of the glut of volunteer fire fighters, the St. Pete clearinghouse used a method that the health care community should emulate in the future. All fire personnel who wanted to volunteer were told to report by phone first to the St. Pete dispatcher. There, if they were needed, they were given a tasking number that corresponded with a specific assignment in South Dade. If a volunteer showed up without the tasking number, he or she was courteously referred back to St. Pete. In this way an objective and uninvolved third party took the pressure off the busy local officials and secured only the help that was needed when and where it was needed.

There was a brief period when the medical profession in South Dade, like the Metro Dade Fire Department, really needed some organized help. That period lasted longer in Florida City than in wealthier areas. But it was over by the time CNN broadcast word of the emergency need for physicians and nurses.

On Wednesday Governor Chiles decided to move the state EOC from Tallahassee to South Florida, to the former Eastern

Airlines office building at Miami International Airport. The first and most important requirement to make the facility operational as an emergency operations center was communications. Unfortunately, the State of Florida had decided that it did not need to pay the additional annual cost of securing priority telephone line reinstallation from Southern Bell in case of emergency. So when the state EOC officials asked for thousands of phone lines by the next day, Southern Bell told them they did not qualify as a top priority. FEMA then set up a satellite phone system that connected the Miami office of the state EOC with the phone service in Baltimore, Maryland. Williams, the state's health care coordinator, recalled what happened next:

> Somehow the number got out. I think CNN released it, saying that if any physician wanted to volunteer, this was the number to call. This was our most abysmal failure—trying to deal with the health volunteers that came in. Metro Fire and Rescue took care of the fire volunteers. I was responsible for all medical volunteers, which includes physicians, nurses, all EMTs, public health nurses, dentists, veterinarians, and anybody else that is construed to have something to do with medical.
>
> The first phone call I got was seconds after the line opened. It was from this man who said, "Young man, I am on my way and I am coming to help. I am the president of the Korean War Doctors Association of America." I said, "Fine, what are you going to do?" He said, "Well, we are going to come down there and save lives." I said, "Sir, to the best of my knowledge we don't have a lot of trauma victims down here. We mostly have a public health crisis." He said, "Dammit, we're coming." I said, "What do you mean, we?"
>
> He said, "I got all 14 members of the association in my Winnebago." I said, "Sir, let me take your number. Please sit tight. We will call you back when we find an appropriate place to use you." And he said, "You don't seem to understand. I just crossed the Florida state line, and I'll be there in four hours, and you better have some place to put me or I am going to set up shop."
>
> This was [typical] of the volunteers that were coming in. Frankly the medical volunteers were coming for guts, gore, and trauma, and every nasty thing that you can imagine, and we had none of that to give them. It just didn't exist. What we needed were some primary care docs.

Down in Florida City, however, the story was different. By Wednesday, the Lee County contingent had established its ad hoc EOC in the remains of the Hampton Inn. The EOC was linked with the Lee County field hospital, which had been set up near city hall. This was the only communication link that existed in the area.

When Elaine Gorman, the Key Largo EMT and trauma specialist, returned to Florida City on Thursday, she and her group of EMT volunteers from Key Largo located the ad hoc EOC at the Hampton Inn and paid a visit to offer assistance. Gorman asked who was in charge of the medical component of the Hampton Inn EOC and, after some hemming and hawing, was informed that she was.

Gorman recounted the Florida City situation, beginning the day after the storm:

> Initially what we did was come back into Florida City on our way back to Monroe. Fire [and rescue] had set up a command post at a McDonalds restaurant. We went back to Monroe County to make sure our district was covered. On Tuesday morning we headed back up with one ambulance. At that time we made contact with some of the [Lee County] field hospital personnel that were just coming in, setting up a tent near where Florida City's city hall had been.
>
> I went out with a group of physicians late on Tuesday to the migrant camp. But it took us a long time, and there were very few people there that we could see. We couldn't explore the camp because everything was torn down and across the road. The trailers were completely flattened. It was the worst devastation that I had seen. We did what we could to provide first aid.
>
> Florida City was extremely isolated, so in actuality we just went back to the Lee County headquarters and worked out of there.
>
> It was about Day Four that I started to realize that there were multiple physicians and nurses setting themselves up on street corners everywhere. Nobody was reporting to anybody. Nobody had any line access to tetanus and some of the things they needed. So I walked into the EOC the Lee County crew had set up, and I said I would like to offer my services to whomever is in charge, the chief medical officers. And they said, "Well, um." And I said, "I beg your pardon, there is no medical organization out there." And they said, "Well, then, it's you."

That's how I ended up becoming medical commander. So we started to try to link up. The National Guard had set up a tent down toward the prison. They were doing outreach, sending out ambulances on a daily patrol through the area. We set up some public health nurses at Everglades neighborhood camp. We had volunteer ambulances from Tampa and Sarasota. I had them go to the tent hospitals and sit, so that when someone came into the tent hospitals and needed transport we were there. The first few days we sent them to James Archer Smith [now South Miami Homestead], until it closed. Then we sent most of them to Baptist. We did mostly primary care, however, treating people whose medicine had run out, the diabetics who had not been able to take their insulin, some primary wound care. There was a lot of tetanus given out, a lot of diarrhea. There was a lot of shooting going on, but we did not do that much in terms of serious injuries, mostly primary care.

Florida City was extremely isolated. It took seven days before we had assistance with water for drinking or cleaning. We were not able to get medicine through any chain. We basically had hospitals from all over the country send stuff directly to us, bypassing the organization north of us. We could not hook into the [official] system. They were not aware that Florida City had a medical command or that they had an EOC going. And I am not sure how that came about. I don't know now who they thought was taking care of Florida City.

We used my car and runners to the Centro Campesino migrant camp, the Lee County tent hospital, and a tent hospital the National Guard had set up, and to a tent set up by Jackson Memorial Hospital staff near the water tower. We had five tents, but everyone was working independently. So what we did was go out and try to find what supplies everyone was short of, then try to get them. Literally, because the communications system had broken down so badly, we had to send out runners.

Gorman said her people in Key Largo and in other areas made telephone contact with hospitals around the country, including hospitals in Seattle and Bowling Green, Ohio, who wanted to help. When told the needs of the volunteers in Florida City, the facilities thousands of miles away were able to send in supplies long before Florida City's rag-tag rescuers could get supplies from the official rescue and recovery operation just 10 miles north.

According to Gorman,

There wasn't much order. We even ended up with multiple units of military. We had Seabees, we had paratrooper-type units, we had regular army, we had National Guard. Not one of those could communicate with each other, radio-to-radio. They all had different radio systems. It was very, very frustrating.

Things came about because people made them come about. But there was no concept of incident command at all, because in order to command you have to be able to communicate.

When Gorman learned that the federal government had set up a pharmacy at the South Dade government center to provide needed medication to field hospitals, she drove up and put in her request. First she was greeted with surprise. "We didn't know you were there. We didn't know anybody was working there," they said. She recalled:

We ran into some real strange situations. We had medications coming through, but they were not coming through legitimately. We became uncomfortable with the process that things were floating through our hands that should not have been. So when I went up to the government center and met with them, we told them that we had these meds, but they were not very secure at the Hampton Inn. They told us about the federal pharmacy at Opa Locka, and we agreed to bring up the excess meds that we had and take them to Opa Locka if the federal pharmacy would go ahead and provide for our tent hospitals. They said fine, we will do a site interview and do the rounds to make sure everything is OK, then we will provide for them and you won't have to. We agreed. But after two days, I found that none of our hospitals in Florida City was getting the medicine they requested from the federal pharmacy.

So I went back up to the government center EOC to find out what was wrong. And I found out we had ended up in a classic Catch 22. They said, "You can't have the medicine." And I said, "Why?" They said, "Well, they're tents." And I said, "Yes?"

They said they could not deliver medicine to those pharmacies down there because they were tents, that medications had to be in a room that could be closed up and locked. I said, "You don't understand. There are no rooms in Florida City, no buildings."

The Hampton Inn was the only two-story building left standing and it was not secure. The irony is they said they were here to help us, they would provide us with everything we needed, and we would no longer have to scramble, scratch, and search, but you can't take medicine to the tents. It was like, the only thing we have are tents.

These people were very frustrated, too, because they were not allowed to do what they wanted to do. Everyone was locked into a command structure that would not allow anyone to make an ultimate decision.

And the problem went beyond medication, according to Gorman:

We needed porta-potties at the migrant center. Everyone knew where there were 100 potties sitting in one place not being used. Everyone agreed that we should have them. But no one had the authority to allow us to get them. And then it took seven days to get these porta-potties to where they needed to be. And then, five days later, when it came time to clean them there was no one in charge of the upkeep of them.

So instead of becoming part of the solution, the potties became part of the problem, because they had overflowed and they were right near the food area, and we had created a hazard, but not for not wanting to try. Everybody promised that they would do everything they could, and they did. But there were so many channels to go through, we were in quicksand all the time.

The Lee County ad hoc EOC was having similar difficulties when its commander ran into Governor Chiles on Thursday in the middle of a field with a contingent of press in tow. The Lee County commander gave the following account of what happened next:

We told him we were doing all we could for the people of Florida City, and he said that was great and told us to keep up the good work and that he was supporting us. We took that to mean we had his authorization to do what we needed. So when we needed telephones at the EOC at the Hampton Inn, we got Southern Bell to go out and find us a pair that worked. They found a pair with a dial tone down the road a few miles along U.S. 1. We told them we needed a hundred pair the next day and that the governor had authorized them to make it happen.

They dug a mile-and-a-half trench all night long and delivered the lines at the Hampton Inn. Then we told the manager of the Hampton Inn we would have to put yet another hole in the one room that wasn't damaged to bring in the wires and set up the phones. He was already upset because we had commandeered his business and evicted all his guests, under the governor's authority, of course. So we told him that, just like with the rooms we commandeered, the governor would pay him for the damage.

The Hampton Inn provided some amount of shelter. It had running water that was not potable but could be used for cleaning. It reeked of mosquito spray, one of the necessities of life at the edge of the drenched Everglades. The mosquito spray, like much of the medicine in the first days after the storm, came from as far away as Seattle. The squadrons of mosquito-control aircraft that covered much of South Dade with batex and malathion did not spray Florida City, as far as Gorman can remember. "There was never any spraying," Gorman said. But then much of what went on in Florida City was, to the officials 10 miles north, a fantasy.

"The authorities from Florida City asked if we could take over, and a lot of money from Lee County and Monroe County was laid out. But essentially afterwards, it was like we were not in the chain. The big EOC did not invite us to come. We were not official," Gorman said.

It was perversely fortunate that the migrants were the ones who were getting the short end of the public health wagon, rather than the more prosperous hurricane victims up north. "I think the reason we did not see more people with diarrhea and other problems related to sanitation was that the people in our area were largely migrants who were used to living under less sanitary conditions and had built up a resistance to bacteria and the germs associated with a loss of water pressure," Gorman said.

In truth, the Florida City hurricane victims probably saw an improvement in their health care after the storm compared with what they were getting before the storm.

Gorman was struck by what she calls the madness that seemed to be everywhere. She recalled,

Somehow it had gotten out to law enforcement that there were baboons around that had escaped from the AIDS research center. On one trip we stopped, and a baboon came up and was kind of hugging my leg. It was clear that he wasn't dangerous or going to hurt anybody. It was clear he was familiar with humans and probably trying to say he was hungry. They took him off to the side of the road and blew his head off. It was very bizarre. He was clearly not a research animal but somebody's pet who thought we were bringing him dinner. To me it underlined the madness that was existing at the time. I mean, nobody was doing it to be mean. Their behavior was not abnormal. It just underlined how bizarre life had become.

Meanwhile, up the road in Homestead and South Dade, where buildings and parts of buildings still remained, where people who had never lived without air conditioning were facing their fourth day without even electricity to power a fan, things were also getting strange.

By August 26, tons of supplies, hundreds of would-be helpers, and a host of agencies were prepared to rush into South Dade—if only they had somewhere to go and a guard to protect them as they went there. Security beyond the military encampments was a real problem, since few buildings that could be locked were left standing and even fewer were solid enough to prevent looting at night and drenching during the day.

Affluent, hard-working people who normally kept tidy yards and were concerned about their neighborhood's appearance, people who, only days earlier, would not have dreamed of covering their homes with graffiti, began spray-painting messages, bon mots, and curses on the remains of homes. Some were openly carrying weapons. So many crimes were being committed that the standing order for the police was to respond only to assaults, murders, and armed robberies that were in progress.

The air reeked with the stench of dead animals, human waste, and soaked fabric. The rains became a curse far worse than the storm itself. A message was sent on Wednesday, Day Three, to President Bush, stating that the National Guard could not control the mob, feed the hungry, rebuild the infrastructure, and police the streets. Within 24 hours the first contingent of federal troops arrived. The total number was 2,000.

Meanwhile, at the state EOC that had relocated to Miami Airport, the FEMA bosses knew that they and their resources were desperately needed, documents show. But they continued to wait for state officials to make a formal request in writing.

A commander of a helicopter group explained his difficulty that first week: "Initially our mission was not real clear. Get to Florida and help out. We like to have a little more information than that."

With pantries empty, spoiled food and body waste melding into a sickening fog, water impossible to find, mosquitoes biting, no help in sight, rain ruining remaining property, looters slinking in the dark, repair materials maliciously overpriced, the victims and their supposed saviors began to get a bit testy.

A new estimate put the storm's toll at 22 dead, 175,000 homeless, 1 million without power, and 63,000 homes destroyed. Kate Hale, drowning in failure, noticed that the one way to get a problem solved in the midst of the chaos was to bring in a live action news team. Within hours, whatever problem the news media highlighted was on its way to being solved.

Bedraggled, exhausted, and frustrated with the melange of agencies trying, but not succeeding, to execute the relief and recovery, Hale called a press conference and insisted that it be carried live. At 10:30 a.m. on Thursday, Day Four, Hale stood on a chair and issued a blunt statement:

> Enough is enough. Quit playing like a bunch of kids. Where the hell is the cavalry? For God's sakes, where are they? We're going to have more casualties because we're going to have people dehydrated. People without water. People without food. Babies without formula. We need food, we need water, we need people down here. We're all about ready to drop, and the reinforcements are not going in fast enough.

Transportation Secretary Andrew Card, Jr., materialized at the Dade EOC within an hour. "Help is on the way," he promised. Four hours later, smugly assuming that the administration was doing everything it could, Card convened a meeting of the federal relief officials assembled in South Florida. The senior FEMA official promised a significant federal presence within a day. Card asked what that meant, and the FEMA official told him there would be not one, but two FEMA disaster assistance centers open the next day.

Card asked how many personnel that would mean.

"Six," the FEMA executive responded.

"Six in each?" Card asked.

"Three in each," was the response Card was given to relay to the president and candidate for reelection.

Twenty thousand troops of the 18th Airborne Division, on standby since Monday, were finally released that evening. At 9:15 the next morning an Army C-5A was on the ground amid the remains of Homestead Air Force Base, disgorging rangers in Humvees to restore order and set up kitchens. Within 24 hours, a million rolls of toilet paper and 4,000 portable toilets were being unloaded on the dock at Dodge Island.

It was the end of the beginning and the beginning of the end.

In the aftermath of natural disaster, water becomes more precious than gold. Dehydration, especially dangerous to the young and to the elderly, is a constant threat when normal supplies are cut off or possibly polluted. At a field kitchen in a park, bottles of water await distribution to some of the 175,000 homeless in South Dade, and to those with homes but not water.

PUBLIC HEALTH PROBLEMS AND ISSUES

The realization that Hurricane Andrew had changed from a trauma-oriented, search-and-rescue mission to a major public health problem came with the discovery that Metro Dade Water and Sewer had overestimated its ability to survive a storm using backup pumps and emergency repairs. The discovery came on Tuesday, Day Two. On Wednesday, Day Three, the Metro Dade government announced that no one south of Coral Reef Drive had running water and none would be available for some time. The system had failed to survive the storm, and its backups had failed to meet the demand.

Water pressure is the critical component of public health in contemporary society. Without pressure, with pipes ripped apart by fallen trees, the entire system in Dade was susceptible to biological contamination. Some in the damaged area had sufficient water to shower or boil. For most, there simply was no water: nothing to drink, boil, wash with, or flush.

Wednesday marked the start of the real health care emergency. And almost immediately the participants who gathered at the South Dade government center in Cutler Ridge for the morning Health Task Force meeting began arguing about the potential problems and their possible solutions. What to do with the rotting bodies of domestic animals? Where and how to get water supplies? How to distribute the water? What about airborne insects? How to combat typhus and cholera? Mike Williams, the state EMS coordinator who established the health EOCs in Tallahassee and then in Cutler Ridge, remembered that the meetings took an average of six hours those first few days and accomplished nothing, since no one was actually in charge of anything except their own little zone of responsibility.

The first systematic attempt to quantify the public health problem was undertaken by two University of Miami physicians, Claudio Cabrejos and Jorge Hermida, members of the university's Field Epidemiology Survey Team (FEST). Their unedited notes demonstrate the problems that were common in all the ad hoc medical facilities and emergency food kitchens. The huge dimensions of the task of providing nourishment and shelter overcame any sense of public health consciousness, despite an awareness on the part of the participants. Their report is remarkable in that it shows how only two people insisting on the basics of public health can make a difference in the face of enormous resistance.

According to their field report, they were tasked "to establish an autonomous but interrelated epidemiology and public health unit in a reference disaster relief center." The objectives included "to inspect, evaluate and assist the basic epidemiology and public health needs of the reference center and inform the other logistical units of it and establish first action priorities." They were to "inform and ask for specific aid from the media."

They were assigned to evaluate and manage the disposal of biohazardous waste and solid waste, evaluate the management of solid waste and basic sanitation facilities, and to make recommendations about food preparation and distribution facilities. The two were also tasked to establish a system for infectious disease control, a system for record keeping, and a health education system. And they were supposed to conduct an "inspection and evaluation of the community needs and environmental conditions of the devastated area."

On Tuesday Cabrejos and Hermida were dispatched by Metro Dade Fire and Rescue to the Cutler Ridge command center. It took them five hours to reach the location "because of the lack of central coordination and organization." When they reached their destination, according to their field report, they found "a basic emergency room rudimentarily built, a truck with medical supplies, a truck with food and water, 25 medical personnel and ambulance transport." The report notes that "the first cases were lacerations, dog bites, and traumas."

What they had found, apparently, was the EMT unit that had been set up prior to the arrival of the DMAT unit. The FEST team was sent south the next day by the director of the field hospital to an ad hoc facility that had been established at Homestead Middle School by volunteers and physicians from the U.S. Public Health Service in conjunction with a Red Cross shelter.

"The disorganization was quite evident," the FEST team wrote. "It was a clinic of 3540 medical personnel, a supplies distribution center for food, clothing, water, and medical aid, with logistical management and services. There was no organization for distribution. The clothing was getting wet in the auditorium. The American Red Cross shelter was divided for elderly, families, and a nursing facility."

The report goes on:

> After making contact with the medical director, Dr. [Jack] Young, the epidemiology and public health component of the center was established with the help of a nurse and supplies coordinator. Biohazardous waste was not being handled properly. No proper containers or bags. No location for that waste. They started using an external debris area to dispose of it. We found children playing in that area and asked for the National Guard to control the area.
>
> In the food preparations area they informed us that they were preparing 7,000 meals a day. We observed that some employees were not wearing gloves. We stressed to them to do it and provided them with gloves. The lines of people waiting for food were too close to solid waste and with external sun exposure. [After our intervention] these lines were changed and the solid waste was handled appropriately in plastic bags.
>
> [In another area] the solid waste was improperly disposed of in boxes and in many sites of the center. We observed flies on food waste. We created a central collection point for garbage disposal and stressed the use of plastic bags.
>
> A record-keeping system was initiated. Approximately 300–350 patients were being seen every day. The first cases were fractures, wounds, traumas, postdisaster syndrome; chronic patients: diabetics, asthmatics, hypertensives asking for medications; dermatitis and rashes in children.

Having made contact with the media, we asked for latrines and a system to maintain them, plastic bags, shoes for children due to the increased number of wounded feet. We started seeing it on Channel 51 and 4.

The report for Thursday shows an improvement:

Sanitary conditions improved. We received 30 portable toilets and gloves. Plastic bags for solid waste were received and distributed. Shoes and general supplies were received, as well as medical supplies. We brought from the university biohazardous waste containers, bags, and labels. We distributed them in the clinic and set up a room with the proper signs outside. We also brought bleach in plastic containers. First cases of gastrointestinal complaints and otitis media were seen.

On Friday the FEST team reported as follows:

Record keeping to identify infectious disease trends. Cases of gastrointestinal and diarrheal diseases on increase. Otitis media in children, contact dermatitis, respiratory problems as well as psychological disorders.

Even before Hurricane Andrew, the public health system in Dade County was in serious trouble. Rates for tuberculosis and AIDS were the second highest in the nation. Health costs were in the upper one third of the nation, while one in four—500,000 residents—had no insurance or too little to make a difference. Almost 40 percent of the newborns in the county suffered some sort of complication at birth. There were at least 25,000 residents with serious mental illness, and 25 percent of Dade residents were not getting the basic health care they needed. In many areas of the county, especially in the poor neighborhoods, citizens waited an average of 11 months after the onset of symptoms before seeing a physician, according to a study of public health issues completed in 1990.

In a letter dated September 11, 1992, Dr. Jack Young detailed the problems facing the public health services and requested about $7 million from FEMA. His comments demonstrated the enormous need that existed even prior to Andrew:

Perinatal health status indicators were examined in 1988, 1990, and 1991 to develop a primary care picture for the target area before Hurricane Andrew struck. The farther south one goes in the target area the poorer the perinatal health outcomes. Such outcomes are associated with the greater amount of poverty that exists in south Dade, in particular target communities. In 1989, less than 30 percent of the 2,200 births to women in [the] Homestead and Florida City area [were] funded by private insurance. One-quarter of the 2,200 deliveries were reimbursed by Medicaid. In Dade County as a whole these figures were 45 percent and 18 percent respectively. The economic plight of low-income persons in this area will only worsen because of the total collapse of the $1-billion nursery industry, the loss of over $400 million related to Homestead Air Base expenditures, the complete termination of tourist activity during the rebuilding phase.

Moreover, within the target area there are a significant number of census tract and/or zip code areas which paint a very stark picture of the health status of families within the target area, even prior to the hurricane. For example, the most densely populated zip code in the target area (33157) had an infant mortality rate of 16.2/1,000 live births in 1989. In 1990, its infant mortality rate, although reduced, was 14.3/1,000. In each of these two years there were more than 1,100 live births to women residing in this zip code. The rate of low-weight births for this zip code in these two years was 9.7 percent and 12.8 percent, respectively. Of the 18 zip codes that comprise the target area, 33 percent had infant mortality rates in excess of 11.7/1,000 live births in 1990.

Young also reviewed immunization status. There, too, the data painted a depressing picture. A 1991 study of first grade children in all of Miami, conducted by the Center for Disease Control (CDC), found only 29 percent had been fully vaccinated by their second birthday. Another CDC study had found that 73 percent of those individuals in the hurricane-affected area who needed medicine had no transportation.

"It was dismal two years ago, and it hasn't gotten any better," Miami Beach mayor Sy Gelber told the media just a few months before Hurricane Andrew. His statement was in response to a plan by the Dade County Public Health Trust to address the problems of primary care for the poor by building yet another hospital in South Dade as part of the Jackson Memorial Hospital system. Other alternatives that were suggested at the time included a decentralization of the health care delivery system through neighborhood clinics that focused on primary care. That recommendation was modified and resubmitted by the Health Planning Council of South Florida with a request for funding from federal disaster sources. Two years after the storm, the plan had not been funded or implemented.

In the wake of Andrew, the residents of far South Dade got a huge dose of free primary care. Some might argue that the previously underserved population of South Dade got an overdose that led to a temporary addiction. As has been described, immediately after the storm the health care community responded with a rush that turned into a stampede.

Unfortunately for the citizens of South Dade, the surge of assistance retreated almost as quickly at it was amassed, leaving them with unfulfilled medical needs, inadequate follow-up care, and raised expectations. The problem of how to wean the medically deprived from their poststorm infusion of help is a major concern that must be addressed for South Florida and other battered regions.

In the short term, however, the unofficial medical relief efforts were about the only hope the indigent had until Kate Hale summoned the military for a dose of benevolent dictatorship. Even then, some opportunities were missed.

The Health Council of South Florida was back in operation within three days after the storm, surveying health service providers in concert with the South Florida Hospital Association and the Office of Licensure and Certification of the Health and Rehabilitative Services. The health council's staff attended the daily meetings of the Health Care Task Force held at the South Dade government center.

By Day Three, health council executive director Linda Quick had identified a facility, the Suburban Medical Center, as a potential site for emergency care that was far cleaner and better equipped than the tent facilities that were being erected around the south end of the county. In a letter to Suburban's director, Dr. Jules Minkes, Quick outlined her efforts to direct officials to the undamaged hospital within their midst:

Within the first three days after the storm, my staff and myself had contacted all of the organized health facilities and programs in South Dade to ascertain their state of functioning. At the same time, my senior staff and I were attending meetings with Doug Cook from the Agency for Health Care Administration, Dr. Jim Howell [then with HRS Health Program Office], Sandra Owen of the Office of Licensure and Certification, Mike Williams of the HRS's Emergency Medical Services, Ellery Gray of the United States Public Health Service, and other state, local, and federal officials working on the recovery response.

Several times in the first few weeks, we mentioned to them that your facility had not been substantially damaged, that you had beds available for use by people in need, and that although licensed as an Ambulatory Surgical Facility, the emergent nature of the situation might make it a more attractive short-term hospital than transporting people out of the area. With each conversation, I was assured that someone would get right on it, until I was finally told that there appeared to no longer be any need for such short-term hospitalization. Specifically, at the point when recognition of the capability of Suburban Medical Center was made, new people necessitating its use were no longer being identified.

Restated briefly, Quick's ramble meant that the need for emergency hospitals had long passed by the time anyone paid attention to the availability of a clean, functioning facility. The moment had come and gone within a week. And it was time to get on with the recovery.

According to Mike Williams, President Bush's designation of Ellery Gray to be the federal public health official in charge marked the turning point in health care delivery to the region. Governor Chiles promptly followed suit by designating Gray as the state public health executive. And, in an abundance of logic, Dade County followed, designating Gray as their man in charge. The unified command worked wonders, however slowly.

Williams also recalled the difference in the length and effectiveness of the daily Health Care Task Force meetings once Gray volunteered to take charge, on Day Five. "We spent six hours and got nothing done. He came in and volunteered to take over the meetings with his flip charts and schedules, and we were out of there in an hour knowing what we were supposed to do," Williams noted.

Walter Livingstone is a veteran in the public health wars. During Andrew he served a number of functions, including director of environmental health in the affected district for the Florida Department of Health and Rehabilitative Services. He was ruthlessly candid in his appraisal of the public health functions immediately after the storm:

> We were unprepared in three particular ways and failed to respond in three ways. We were not prepared to dispose of human waste with the water problems to preclude the flies and the diseases flies can carry. We could not provide temporary shelter. The Pan American Health Organization recommends that people be allowed the opportunity to remain on their own property. We could not do this, but we are looking for something that can be dropped on the doorstep to provide temporary shelter and easily installed. The other problem was hand-washing facilities. We had very few except at the tent cities [which were not open until late in the second week]. This is the most important way to prevent the spread of gastrointestinal illness. And we did not deploy adequate washing stations.

He said the advent of the large tent cities reduced the problems of delivering water and food and locating hand-washing facilities. But the tent cities had the same trash and sanitation problems that any other concentration of humans can create.

"When the military came into play here and set up our famous tent cities, the need was also immediately present for some means of disposing of and removing waste. Porta-potties were an essential part of our emergency response," Livingstone recalled. "Trash and garbage were a continual problem."

The garbage glut resulted in a need for fly control, he said:

> The enormous quantities of organic debris spread around by the storm—with every home, with every refrigerator, every little grocery store, every food warehouse, every supermarket destroyed—created a problem. Then, with the animal carcasses and the human waste, we had a wonderful fly-breeding machine with the warm weather and the rain.
>
> We tried control with baits around the feeding station, but that was totally inadequate. Electric light traps were a drop in the bucket.

What we are proposing for the future does the same that was done in Desert Storm. That is to utilize fly traps in great numbers. They are very cheap to build and easy to stockpile. This proved to be very effective in Desert Storm.

With the arrival of the military, the pest-management system went into combat mode, as Livingstone recounted:

We brought in the specialized military units from the Armed Forces Pest Management Corps, the preventive medicine team from the disease control center in Jacksonville Naval Air Station, and they worked with the Metro Dade Mosquito Control. They helped establish the need for the U.S. Air Force Reserve Aerial Spray Corps. They reduced the population of biting mosquitoes by about 95 percent. But we did that for humanitarian reasons, not disease control.

Livingstone said that since the storm he has located a kind of portable personal commode that he expects will help greatly with sanitation problems in the future. The product consists of a cardboard base with a plastic liner that is biodegradable. In areas with a low water table, the bags can be sealed and buried. In places with a high water table, such as South Florida, where the drinking water supply lies less than a yard below the surface in many places, the bags can be collected for disposal in another location.

No sanctuary was left in the wake of Andrew, both figuratively and literally. Yet, prayer and giving-of-thanks survived, although eight folding chairs and a pulpit were all that remained where once a church stood. Even where all else had crumbled, faith nevertheless stood strong, and good works continued as thousands followed the Golden Rule.

HOW DO YOU SPELL RELIEF?

By August 27, Day Four, the Federal Emergency Management Administration was in place, issuing emergency
checks for food, shelter, and medical needs, including prescriptions. The rush to find emergency housing for volunteers had
already created a shortage of hotel and motel rooms in Dade
County. With the infusion of FEMA funds, the shortage of housing extended to apartments and rental homes as far north as
Palm Beach County.

The outpouring of relief aid was nothing short of spectacular.
By August 27, Anheuser-Bush had donated $1 million, as had
Humana Hospital Corporation. Second Harvest Food Bank in
Orlando had sent 56,000 meals designated for the Red Cross
shelters. Publix Food Stores had donated 22,000 one-gallon bottles of water. AT&T had donated $100,000. Zephyrhills Company
had sent 200,000 cases of bottled water. Xerox Corporation had
sent copy machines, work stations, and fax machines to emergency centers. Motorola had sent 1,500 walkie-talkies capable of
connecting 750 people to each other within a radius of three miles.

McDonalds and Pizza Hut had opened field units in South
Dade that became more popular than the MaRE (meals almost
ready to eat) kitchens 100 yards away. The Florida Dairymen's
Association had sent 50,000 gallons of water. Texaco had sent two
tankers of gasoline, a truck filled with water, and one truck filled
with food. The Naples (Florida) Fire Department had sent 10,000
gallons of water. The government of Taiwan had sent $100,000,

and the U.S. Department of Agriculture had sent nine trucks full of food and water.

The disorganized rush of relief workers and people bringing supplies into South Dade created massive traffic problems as their vehicles mingled with those of newly homeless South Dade residents attempting to go back and forth from their temporary homes in North Dade and Broward County.

To bring some order to the relief effort, community leaders in Dade County established an organization called We Will Rebuild to serve as the consensus agency where cash donations could be channeled, then spent. Governor Chiles established the Florida Relief Center at the fairgrounds in West Palm Beach, where relief supplies could be accepted, sorted, and routed to the appropriate destinations. Among the supplies that were donated were a substantial number of winter sweaters and a few sets of ice skates. In many cases, the clothing that was donated was so fouled with mold, dirt, and parasites, the volunteers who worked sorting out the clothing broke out in contact dermatitis and insect bites. In the end, much of it was burned for fear of infestation.

For the stricken hospitals, the need for water was desperate. August and September in Florida are extremely hot and humid. Few buildings built since 1950, when air conditioning came into popular use, have adequate ventilation to keep them cool by opening windows and doors. Mold and algae spread with amazing speed in the moist, hot environment.

Immediately after the storm, Mt. Sinai Hospital needed 100,000 gallons of water just to restart its air conditioning system. Baptist Hospital needed a similar amount to refill its water tower so the toilets at the hospital could be flushed. While the Baptist staff and their families waited for the precious water, they used a bucket brigade, transporting water from a nearby swimming pool to flush the hospital's toilets. The Baptist toilets had been installed with water-saving Flush-O-Meters to match demand with supply when supply was abundant. On Tuesday, August 25, when the Baptist engineering department secured a truckload of water to fill the tower, a wave of relief spread through the hospital. But the relief quickly subsided. The Flush-O-Meters on the toilets were all in their open positions as the water entered the tower. Pressure was never sufficiently established, and the water simply flowed through the system nonstop and out into the sewer system.

The irony of the water crisis is that South Dade has thousands of shallow and deep water wells. It was once an agricultural area, where farmers grew hundreds of acres of mangoes, avocados, decorative plants, and vegetables. It did not become part of the county sewer system until the last decade, so it relied on wells for potable water and agricultural water, and it relied on wells and septic tanks for waste disposal. Yet no effort was made to put emergency generators on pumps that were already in place to water lawns and fill swimming pools and thereby draw water directly from the ground. Well water, however poor its quality, could have been used for hand washing, cooling, and toilet flushing. A generator, a pump, and some hoses could have saved tens of thousands of people from discomfort and the risk of illness. But no one seized this initiative, assuming, instead, that the water that had not been contaminated by a century of septic tanks would be contaminated by a few days' worth of rotting animal and vegetable life.

In addition to the problems caused by the lack of water, all the hospitals in the affected area suffered from the continued loss of power. All had emergency generators, but not sufficient enough to power lights, medical equipment, critical refrigeration, the kitchens, and the air conditioners. Computer-controlled equipment, especially in the laboratories, was no longer dependable for critical tests. The generators required huge amounts of fuel, and none of the hospitals had planned to be on generator power a week after the storm. Each of Baptist's four generators burns 2,000 gallons of diesel fuel in 24 hours, for example.

At Baptist, the emergency room patient load tripled. The hospital housed 900 patients, staff, and family members. The Baptist kitchen—which fed 300 on an average day, when it had complete power for refrigeration, water, and ovens—was feeding an average of 800 people at each sitting after the storm. At Jackson Memorial Hospital, the crush of patients and families, when added to the large staff in attendance after the storm, overburdened the limited resources in the cafeteria.

Jackson required its employees to pay for their food. That led to food fights among the medical staff and other employees, some of whom insisted on being fed before the indigent patients, who were, after all, not paying their own way. It took an executive order to resolve the dispute in favor of the patients, thereby assuring that patients would be fed before anyone on staff.

The shortage of water and power created a desperate need for clean linens, sheets, towels, and gowns at all the hospitals, since the laundries could not function at anywhere near capacity—when they could function at all.

Water, fuel, food, laundry, medicine, gases, dressings: the moral of the story is that medical facilities cannot function after a destructive event such as a hurricane without strong relationships with their vendors and suppliers. Many times, as in the case of Hurricane Andrew, strong relations may not even be enough.

Less than a month after Andrew, the South Florida Hospital Association reviewed the most common problems experienced by its member hospitals. Water was one of the most pressing problems, and the association recommended the drilling of six- to eight-inch-diameter wells. The association also noted that hospitals that had negotiated contracts with water suppliers had underestimated their needs by up to 200 percent. It recommended that hospitals review their planned requirements and triple the estimate when negotiating with suppliers. They also suggested making arrangements with a backup supplier for water—a good idea for all critical material—at some distance from the facility in need, since many of the supply facilities in South Florida were destroyed.

Compensation was also a concern. Hospitals that used payroll services that operated off campus had little difficulty with payroll. Those that produced the payroll in house had substantial problems, both with accuracy and timeliness in making the payroll cycles.

The question of compensation from Medicare for patients who had been evacuated from one hospital to another was quickly solved by Richard L. Warren, the regional administrator for Medicare. On August 26, 1992, he issued this ruling:

> The following special billing guidelines will apply to services provided Medicare beneficiaries who were evacuated due to Hurricane Andrew.
>
> In situations where Medicare beneficiaries were evacuated

from one hospital to another hospital, the originating hospital should bill from admission to final discharge as though the patient was never moved. It will be the responsibility of the two providers involved in the evacuation to resolve the financial issue of payment for services rendered by the receiving hospital during the evacuation period, as the originating hospital will receive the full Medicare reimbursement for covered services.

There should be no discharges or transfers from the originating hospital to the receiving hospital unless the patient was ultimately discharged from the receiving hospital during the evacuation period. If a patient was discharged from the receiving hospital prior to a transfer/move back to the originating hospital, the normal prospective payment procedures apply to those hospitals reimbursed under the prospective payment system. The originating hospital should transfer the beneficiary to the second hospital. The receiving hospital should follow normal admission procedures and file the discharge claim.

Charges for ambulance transportation will be paid according to the usual reimbursement guidelines. Ambulance transportation charges for patients who were evacuated from and returned to originating hospitals should be included on the inpatient claims submitted by the originating hospitals. Payment will be included in the DRG reimbursement amounts made to hospitals paid under the prospective payment system. Outpatient claims may be submitted for ambulance charges incurred by those patients who were transported from the originating hospitals and subsequently discharged by receiving hospitals.

Evacuation from nursing facility to nursing facility or to hospital:

In situations where a beneficiary receiving a skilled level of care is evacuated from one nursing facility to another nursing facility or from a nursing facility to a hospital, there should be no discharge. The originating nursing facility should bill the claim for a covered skilled level of care as normal. The nursing facility or hospital receiving the evacuated patient should bill the originating provider for services rendered.

In a case where a patient was an inpatient in a nursing facility and not receiving a skilled level of care and the patient was evacuated and admitted to a hospital, the situation should be treated as an admission and must be reviewed by the PRO individually to determine the medical necessity of the admission. Waiver of liability would be applied as usual, based on the medical necessity criteria for any denied admission.

Admission from home setting to hospital or nursing home:

In some situations, patients either under a physician's general care or who were receiving covered home health services may have been admitted to a hospital or nursing facility due to the evacuations or conditions resulting from the hurricane; for example, a patient who otherwise would not have been admitted required admission because he or she was dependent on special equipment that did not function due to the loss of electricity. The medical review entity must determine case-by-case the medical necessity of each admission. The usual billing procedures will apply relative to billing ambulance services.

As described in Chapter 12, the most urgent need in South Dade after the hurricane was for a consolidated delivery system that included primary and secondary health care, mental health services, and access to such social services as legal aid and food stamps. There were many facilities in place to dispense medication and social services. But transportation—getting people to the places that were dispensing what services were available—was a major challenge after the hurricane. Even the affluent had difficulty, because of the destruction of vehicles. For the less affluent, who perhaps had lost a vehicle or were confronted with a failed public transportation system, the need to get around was desperate. The poor needed food and water and medicine and a way to get to the various agencies that offered relief.

Charles Johnson, a publicist for several cab companies, normally remains dispassionate about his clients; but he spoke with pride about the volunteer army of minivan drivers and their accomplishments in setting up the remarkable system that emerged in response to the transportation needs of South Dade:

As South Dade reeled from the blows inflicted by Hurricane Andrew, a group of county administrators and private transportation executives met and in hours put together a disaster relief transportation service that became one of the great but little-known success stories of the recovery from the killer storm.

Within 66 hours, the first van of what was to become a fleet of 260 privately owned and operated vehicles was out on debris-clogged streets, pioneering a program that is now being viewed as a model for other communities facing a similar disaster.

In Andrew's wake relief officials set to work. The military moved in. Storefront clinics opened. Tent cities and tent hospitals sprang up. Distribution centers for food, water, clothing, and other emergency supplies went into operation. But hundreds of thousands of people had no way to reach these centers.

By Friday after the Monday hurricane, FEMA had obligated $45.8 million dollars to the Metro Dade Transit Authority to provide emergency transportation. That same day, the minivans of Miami started running on 12 routes. By the next Tuesday, the number of vans had grown to 140. Within a week, 180 vans and buses were running 16 hours a day on two shifts, with 300 drivers participating.

The system was organized by a coalition of Metro and private companies, including Mayflower Transportation Services, Red Top, Airocar, and Handi-van. Most of the drivers had been involved in airport service, and some had experience driving disabled individuals. Few of them knew South Dade well enough to follow directions, especially with all the street signs and traffic lights destroyed. So the volunteer supervisors and dispatchers set up a cellular phone dispatch system and marked the routes with stripes of yellow paint. There were not enough cellular phones to go around, however, so the drivers had to try to find working phones along their routes from which to call the dispatchers.

The fleet of vans and jitneys operated 16 hours a day, free of charge to users. It became an invaluable service for all the residents of South Dade and a lifeline for the neediest residents. Drivers were willing to pick up stranded homeowners and take them to important meetings with attorneys or insurance agents, as well as get workers to work and families to the food kitchens and health care facilities. The service averaged 20,000 boardings a day. Without it, any effort to provide public health or mental health relief would have been impossible.

Beyond the service for the general public, 6,000 disabled and elderly hurricane victims were transported each day by the 66 vehicles and drivers that had been assigned to the 40 nonprofit and social service organizations who participated in HANDS, the

Hurricane Network Dispatch System. HANDS got dialysis patients to treatment. The system carried an average of 300 frail elderly a day to meals and medical care. Another 300 daily riders were carried to job-training programs where they learned skills needed to help rebuild South Dade.

Most of the vehicles in the disaster transportation system were owner-operated, and many had been operating at the edge of legality. But the coalition required all of the vehicles to pass safety inspections. The drivers were required to have valid licenses, and the entire fleet was covered by a blanket liability policy. Since the vans were running without charge to passengers, a salary rate of $16.50 an hour was established for the drivers. Spanish-speaking drivers made up 65 percent of the work force. African American drivers represented 35 percent, but many of those counted as African American were actually Haitian immigrants.

Metro Dade Transit Authority printed 300,000 fliers telling about the disaster transportation system in three languages and distributed them through the FEMA-funded facilities, the tent cities, and the health care system. Because there was no power and no television in much of South Dade for a month after the storm, the jitney drivers, whose ethnicity approximated the cultural mix and language abilities of the riders, became the messengers and interpreters of the relief effort, as well as its transportation backbone.

This system grew spontaneously and in response to a very real dilemma. Before the hurricane, the jitneys had been operating without licenses and regulation in pockets of poverty, competing with the Metro Dade Transit buses. The ad hoc system worked as well as it did because the jitneys were, in almost all ways, a reflection of the community.

As other communities prepare emergency plans, they ought to consider including many of the elements that occurred spontaneously in the transportation coalition's emergency system and the HANDS system. The following are some recommendations:

- Keep the routes fluid.
- Respond to calls.
- Task a set of vans to social service agencies for exclusive use.
- Match the drivers to the demographics of their routes.

- Teach the drivers the basics of public health and the transportation system. Use them to spot people at risk passing through their area.
- Put public health nurses or aides on the buses and vans at certain intervals to monitor what is happening beyond the treatment centers.
- Integrate the emergency transportation system into the public health and mental health relief roles by using the buses and vans as rumor control devices and as places to dispense and collect important health care information.

Thousands of passengers were stranded at airports, where the lack of power made normal activities impossible and "airborne" took on new meaning for planes parked on the tarmac and in hangars. Tossed like matchsticks, airplanes rest in a jumbled mess. The wind gauge at the National Hurricane Center broke at 164 miles per hour.

A UNIQUE OPPORTUNITY

When Hurricane Andrew wiped out the physical landscape of South Florida, it leveled the health care landscape as well, providing an opportunity and a challenge to start over again, especially in the delivery of primary care.

Andrew destroyed or severely damaged the few public health care centers that were already in place, including the Perrine, Doris Ison, and Martin Luther King health centers. In their place, ad hoc health care facilities, which became known as "doc-in-a-box," blossomed in store fronts and trailers. But they wilted as the damaged traditional systems emerged from the shambles and returned to action. With their expectations raised by the sudden outpouring of medical assistance, the poor among the hurricane victims flocked to hospitals and clinics for follow-up care and the treatment of the wide range of traumas that are inevitable during extended hurricane clean-up.

As the frustrations that followed the storm ramified, anger built within the victims without an appropriate vent. Guilt, fear, loss, and anguish dominated their emotions, creating a festering psychological sore that no one was prepared to treat, let alone prevent. The need for psychological outreach grew exponentially among the residents.

Into the mix of victims and rescuers came highly paid but uninsured construction workers and their families, who put enormous demands on the already stressed health and mental health delivery system. The reconstruction workers' mission was essen-

115

tial to the rebuilding. Their needs were real and their right to access the local health care system undeniable. Yet their unpaid medical bills were not regarded as a consequence of the hurricane and therefore were not eligible for federal underwriting. Because of this, Homestead/SMH Hospital, which treated many of them as walk-ins at its emergency room, was forced to go to the state to offset $18 million in unanticipated costs associated with post-storm clients.

South Dade County was lavished with free health care immediately after the storm. Plans were announced to continue rehabilitation of the area and its people far into the future. They were not unlike competing plans that had been promulgated before the storm. Everyone had a plan to help the underserved population of rural South Dade.

If all the good intentions for the delivery of health care to South Dade were turned into plates and stacked on top of each other, they would fall over. Before the storm, South Dade had been a political arena where the Dade Public Health Trust and the officials of Jackson Memorial Hospital practiced variations on the theme of primary care and public assistance. It was a pocket of poverty that was projected as a target of future growth with a more affluent population. As such, it was an area coveted by the commercial hospitals operating in the area. They were opposed to the construction or expansion of competing hospital facilities, especially the planned opening of a branch of Jackson Memorial. Jackson and its parent political organization, the Dade County Public Health Trust, on the other hand, felt Jackson ought to enter the South Dade market.

The Health Council of South Florida, a state-funded advisory panel, had proposed a community-based primary care system for South Dade that would expand existing services without any need for additional bricks and mortar. The plan excluded new hospital facilities by either Jackson Memorial or by commercial hospitals. The Health Council concept focused on prevention and early intervention, especially among children and pregnant women. After the storm the Health Council integrated its proposal into a plan to rebuild the South Dade health care delivery system and submitted the plan to the Public Health Trust. More than two years after the storm, the proposal remained unanswered.

Perhaps the most successful interim program spawned by Andrew was the mental health and social service delivery program established by Sara Herald. Herald, an attorney and pro bono advocate for children and families, assumed the unfilled position of disaster relief coordinator for the Alcohol, Drug Abuse, and Mental Health section at the Florida Department of Health and Rehabilitative Services (HRS) District XI.

Since the agency had no plans for posthurricane service, she assembled a team of social workers, public health nurses, psychologists, and volunteers and launched a door-to-door program that became the embodiment of successful outreach. Her teams stayed in the same neighborhoods, tracking the progress of the same families, providing preventive help that ranged from public assistance to drug counseling to family planning.

According to Kate Hale, the outreach function was critical in the first seven days after the storm. But in Herald's estimation, the only outreach function performed during the first two weeks after the storm was ad hoc, disorganized, and uncompensated.

Evelena Bestman, a psychologist on the teaching faculty at the University of Miami, recalled that a group of psychologists who had been organized by the National Association for Psychology arrived in South Florida within the first week after Andrew, the first time any such effort on the part of mental health professionals had been attempted. "Pre-Andrew, mental health had a slow evolution into the disaster arena," Bestman recalled. "This is the first time, maybe in history, that mental health was put into the disaster relief program. We were given a real presence. But the key question is, What is mental health in disasters? People are still wondering what mental health in disasters really means, because most people associate mental health with psychology and psychiatry," she said. And she praised the efforts of Herald and her group:

> I am one of the strongest admirers of the team that Dade County put into effect, because it shows that the anguish, the anger, and the pain cannot be put into a little square piece of paper called mental health. It is the combination of so many factors of what people are going through.
>
> This has been the problem of most states pre-Andrew. So in most states planning doesn't exist. You look at the mock drills. They have people covered with catsup who lie there, and they

practice with them. But nobody has a protocol for questions about what have they gone through. Then you follow through, after a few months, to find out what happens to the citizens, and there is no data, there is no research. It is an area that very, very slowly is emerging.

We do know an awful lot about what happens to people in general terms. We do know how to help. But we are not putting it into action. But one agency that is doing it is the Red Cross. The Red Cross finally has a mental health component within its system. They have a very good profile for mental health assistance.

But Bestman cautioned that these worthwhile first steps are not sufficient, nor do they compare favorably with the system developed by Herald and her team:

Post-Andrew there is a great need to anticipate mental health issues at the state, county, and local levels, and that does not exist. We did not anticipate and prepare way back before Andrew, not even a week before Andrew. And what is the anticipation based on? Knowledge.

There is a relationship between the impact area and the amount of consequence you are going to have for mental health. There is a difference between working in the first month and the sixth month. People will be doing trial and error.

There [is] a tendency to call [the problems that people suffer after a disaster] "postdisaster dysfunction." [The problems] don't stop at the moment people answer the questioners. [We are in] a process of planning and learning and training. The whole field of mental health is an evolutionary field. We are a bit primitive; but in Dade County, it is moving because of what Sara Herald is doing; her model comes closer to what we need to be thinking of.

Herald recalled her introduction to mental health and social services, government style:

I was working on getting aid for foster kids and getting foster kids relocated and the stuff that I normally do. And I got a call, two weeks poststorm. I got a desperate phone call to come in and be the disaster relief coordinator. Does that kind of tell you the kind of planning that we had going on for alcohol, drugs, or mental health? There was no plan. And the federal government couldn't find anybody at the state level or at the county level that was in charge in alcohol or mental health. So what you had was a whole bunch of very well-meaning individuals and group social services and community-based organizations and university personnel and doctors and psychologists and counselors that were coming into town, and absolutely no coordination.

And the irony of this is that the only stream of funding, at the federal level, that is absolutely guaranteed in the case of a natural disaster is money for mental health. Can you believe, it is the only one that anybody could have told you, six months before the hurricane, that you were going to get [a grant for] after a hurricane? It is a recognized part of the Stafford Act; therefore, everyone could have been guaranteed mental health services if we had had a plan.

Number one, you need a plan, and you don't do the plan after. But we did. And the only thing I can tell you that qualified me for the job is that I am very good on my feet and I have a background in community-based planning, and I believe in listening to what people need and not dictating what they need or what they want. So one of things that we did not do in the planning process is that we did not jump in and say, "I'm here. I am the disaster lead coordinator."

We decided not to spend the money until we polled the community individuals who knew something about what should be done, before we spent millions of dollars.

Without an established plan, Herald decided to create a plan that would have the support of the agency personnel required to make it a success. This took time and, in a sense, postponed the receipt of the coveted grant funds. As Herald recalled,

I can't tell you the number of people who said, "Let's spend it, it's just sitting there. If we don't use it we don't get any more." Unfortunately, I am not a bureaucrat, and I did not have any plan [for] keeping my job, so I did what I thought was right and I said no.

I brought in people like Evelena Bestman, over 150 people who provide substance abuse and mental health services, both in the public and private sectors, and we developed a plan for the community health team. We took a holistic approach. Most of the people we were dealing with were well. They were not mentally ill. They were well, but they were having to deal with extraordinary stress. And if you help them create linkages and let them vent to you and get crisis counseling done at their door, then you reduce the risk that they will become mentally ill. The nursing factor is there because primary health problems become mental problems if [people] cannot get primary health services. Environmental health is there because we all need to work together to make sure we are not decompensated.

As a veteran of state and federal entitlement programs, Herald looks upon the fruits of public assistance programs as entitlements. Those who are entitled to the "compensation" that helps alleviate their problems are considered "decompensated" when they do not get it, and they can be "decompensated" by the mere fact that they are not aware of their entitlement.

Herald reviewed the mental health system that was in place when she came on the scene:

There was a plan for the mentally ill, but the population with mental illness was very poorly sheltered. They were not cared for in shelters. There were no nurses, counselors, psychiatric nurses, or mental health workers. This is OK if you are only going to be there for a day. But they weren't; they were there longer. And even when tons of pharmaceuticals were brought in, there was not any mental health medication in the pharmacy at the time. We [were] still having trouble six months later because the mental health centers that serve the indigent populations had already exhausted all of their money for medication.

You had people who got prescriptions for $60 medication, then they could not get the medication and they were decompensated. Then how did we treat them? We put them in a crisis stabilization unit at significantly higher cost than the sixty bucks the medication would have cost. We are paying [for] the hospital or Medicare or whatever they qualified for, because we did not get them the $60 they needed to function. They need to be sheltered and medicated so that they can remain stable at a time when there is a greater likelihood that they will be decompensated anyway.

Herald warned that the system of applying for government assistance can be daunting:

I was dealing with six agencies that have some role in disbursement of money that Congress allocated. All had a different set of rules. They had different review criteria. We had people sitting in Vermont reviewing our grant applications, asking questions like, What plans do you have for housing the homeless?

And Herald warned that dire consequences can befall grant recipients who don't keep good books. "You need a single audit trail and a different set of accounting procedures depending on which agency you are dealing with. And if you do not do it right, they can ask you for a refund as long as four years later, depending on the audit procedures."

She also pointed out that it can be difficult to get aid from the state when the state is relying on funding from the federal government:

> Florida's constitution prohibits deficit spending. I had 600 people in the field working for 45 days without contracts because nobody at the state level would let me hire anybody. The staff did it because they had faith that I would sue [the federal government] on their behalf. But you cannot count on leaps of faith in managing people for 60 days at a whack while you wait for the state to contract.

Herald also suggested that the state not only waive the normal requirements for purchasing and bidding but also let the agency that pays the bills know that the change has been made. She said she waited six months to get the state's permission for desperately needed computers.

Her final recommendation was for coordinated emergency planning that is holistic and includes social service delivery. "I recommend a master plan that is integrated to include social services delivery and neighborhood-based organizations. Beyond that, make sure you can take care of yourself and your family. Do not wait for the government to respond."

AFTERWORD

Two anniversaries have passed since the original manuscript for this book was begun. At the first anniversary, I wrote a special section for the South Florida Business Journal, *which is reprinted below. After the second anniversary, I visited Kate Hale, Dade County's emergency manager, to discuss the county's progress. Our conversation is recorded in the second article below.*

It is remarkable how the urgency has waned. That ennui should be a warning to all emergency and medical personnel who must serve in the path of natural disasters. Planning must be a rational, deliberate process and should not rely on emotions. Emotions too often cool before solutions are accomplished.

One Year Later
August 24, 1993

The numbers were staggering.

Sixteen billion dollars—16,000 million dollars—in property damage was committed during only four hours of Andrew's passage.

It has taken the nation of Botswana a hundred years to grow a gross domestic product in excess of $16 billion; likewise, Guatemala and Bangladesh.

And yet, in four hours, Hurricane Andrew cut a swath through South Dade that would cost $16 billion to repair or replace at 1992 prices: an entire year's production by many of the world's nations, gone in a whoosh.

At one point in time, in late August 1992, there were more homeless people in South Dade than in the entire rest of the nation—more than 270,000 homeless, overnight. A million people who had never gone an hour without air conditioning or flush toilets were rammed into a third world existence for more than two weeks.

The numbers were staggering. But what is more significant is that the people still are staggering in the storm's aftermath and 12 months have already passed.

Neither the victims nor their supposed saviors have recovered. Even the ancient pines are suffering from stress. With their nerves ajangle, the trees cannot produce sap and are being consumed by beetles.

And this storm, we have been told, was not the big one. It was too dry.

The federal government has had a year to evaluate its performance during Andrew and take steps to improve it. But a new FEMA law awaits preliminary consideration. No one expects passage until 1994.

Florida's hysterical insurance industry is operating with a gun to its head, dropping policies, begging to get out of town. The risks are too great.

The Red Cross has not recovered from the fury of Hurricane Andrew. It was still short of funds and volunteers when the Mississippi Valley "flood of the century" drained the national organization dry.

In South Florida, where thousands of specially trained volunteers are needed to make today's hurricane plan work, fewer than a thousand are on hand at the anniversary date of Andrew.

But the ultimate toll of Andrew is yet to be reckoned.

Few died in the storm. Those thousands who stayed home during the storm—who experienced their homes being peeled away until nothing came between them and Andrew but a mattress—they will not stay home next time, the experts say. They are going to head out of town or into shelters. Neither the highway system nor the shelters are ready for their potential numbers.

Kate Hale, the Dade County emergency planner, is frightened about the next close encounter. She predicts chaos on the roads and chaos in the shelters. She is urging people to find shelter with friends or family who live on high ground in safe homes.

"Don't rely on the government," she warns.

Two Years Later
September 9, 1994

Two years and two weeks after Andrew departed South Florida, I visited Dade County Emergency Manager Kate Hale at her Southwest Dade bunker.

Tropical Storm Debbie was a new red smudge on Hale's office plotter. Hale was sore from the previous night's yoga class, her first extracurricular activity since Andrew put her on the map. FEMA hats and EMT helmets gathered dust atop her second-hand bookcase.

Apart from that—and Hale's uninvited celebrity—little has been done to improve public safety or public health in the wake of Andrew. Hale, outspoken as ever, made little effort to put a good face on the situation. For an hour she recited the false starts and missed opportunities of the previous two years.

"I am really disappointed in the lack of progress in resolving the issues of special-needs individuals and medical facility preparedness," she said.

Only Baptist Hospital, among the area's major medical facilities, has developed a viable plan to move patients before the arrival of a storm. Only Baptist has devised a plan to assure backup medical staff if the hospital is again the target of a major storm, she said. She recommended that other interested hospitals get a copy of the Baptist "dash" plan and emulate it.

"The local hospitals simply do not want to risk the potential litigation of moving patients to another facility. What if they lose a patient in transit, then the storm warning proves to be a false alarm? They don't want to take the legal risk. I can understand their concerns. But I must still insist that they evacuate and not wait until the last minute like they did during Andrew," Hale said.

The local chapter of the American Red Cross has refused steadfastly to accept special-needs patients into its shelters or to provide any medical assistance to evacuees beyond basic first aid, she said. This means the county must provide a separate network of shelters and find staff to handle the evacuees with special needs.

The county does not want to assign emergency medical technicians to the Red Cross shelters, as it did during Andrew. "The reserve EMTs are needed to reinforce the staff that is in the field during and immediately after a storm," she said.

At present there is no plan to provide medical assistance to any shelters. In the community-spirited afterglow of Andrew, several hospitals promised to "adopt" a nearby hurricane shelter and staff it during a storm. But those promises have been forgotten.

The local medical associations have decided there is no need to plan a way to organize the tide of volunteer physicians who will inevitably follow the next storm. Thoughts of staging physicians just beyond reach of the storm's chaos have been abandoned. Ironically, virtually no physicians or nurses have volunteered to assist in staffing emergency shelters during the next storm. A debate continues whether the county and state can, as a last resort, require state-employed medical personnel to work at the shelters.

Meanwhile, preliminary studies indicate the Andrew experience has dramatically increased the number of people who will seek government-sanctioned shelter. The number is now expected to exceed 100,000.

There are not adequate facilities in South Florida to shelter 100,000 healthy storm victims. But those in greatest need of shelter will not be healthy. Each year the median population grows older, augmenting the potential demand for special care.

The county does not have the resources to house, feed, and provide medical care for tens of thousands of elderly, along with the blind, disabled, mentally ill, and pregnant. Nor does the county have the ambulances to transport the ever-growing numbers. Since the Red Cross will not take anyone with medical problems at its shelters, the only place for those people to go during and after a storm is to family, friends, or hospitals. But Hale wants to close most of the hospitals on Miami Beach and several of the major hospitals that were built in flood zones on the mainland.

Hale said that the Florida legislature responded with knee-jerk speed after Andrew to pass laws requiring hospitals to develop better hurricane evacuation plans and to retrofit existing buildings with shutters and other basic storm protection measures. Few hospitals responded to the new laws. Now, she said, "There is a groundswell of lobbying to water down the law. Excuse the pun. The hospitals claim they can't afford it and don't need it." She predicted the law would be diluted.

Hale said the county office of emergency management has been left out of the planning process for hospital and nursing home preparedness and has no authority to review their plans.The State of Florida is still developing its emergency response plan, Hale said. But as far as she can tell, the state plans to conduct emergency management without the advice or consent of the local government emergency planners.

When floods struck the Florida panhandle in the spring of 1994, Hale was invited by the state to join an evaluation team and witness the efforts to deal with the aftermath.

"They left us waiting at the airport for several hours until we were finally told they had changed their minds and did not feel a need for representatives of the urban counties," she said.

Hale said the decision in the wake of the floods was ironic, since she has spent the majority of her time since Andrew warning anyone who will listen that Andrew was not the big one. She said insiders among emergency planners have counted their blessings that Andrew chose to come ashore at the one spot on the coast of the United States with the least dense population.

South Dade is primarily an agricultural area, interspersed with vast tracts of single-family housing. There are not cities, per se, just small towns. Development extends only five miles inland from the ocean. Beyond and to the west for 60 miles, the storm crossed only the Everglades as it made its way into the Gulf of Mexico. Any other landfall would have targeted at least one significant city and millions more people, Hale said.

"Andrew hit the one place on the coast of the United States where it could do the least damage. If it had hit anywhere else or if it had traveled slower, dumping more rain, then it might have been the big one," she said.

"The real danger in South Florida, with its antiquated flood control system and its enormous residential development at the edge of the Everglades, is that a really wet storm will hit the area," she said. "Then there will be flooding so bad a person could go from Biscayne Bay to Fort Myers [on Florida's west coast] by boat."

In this scenario, the flood control gates that are now opened and closed to keep the residential areas in the western parts of the county from returning to the swamp, will become like dams, holding back the flood flow, spilling the canal systems over their banks and drowning the region.

Hale said the flood control system was designed in the 1940s, specifically to deal with the flooding that occurred after each of the nine hurricanes that hit South Florida in that decade.

"Back then, there were only a few hundred thousand people living along the coast. Now we have 2.5 million people living in areas that were once under water. It was drained for the farmers, who sold it to the developers, who sold it to the public," Hale said. "The system is hopelessly inadequate for true flood control. But nobody seems to be listening."

Hale said she is attempting to develop an emergency plan for the next wet hurricane, but, as is the case with most of her efforts, politics and economics seem to get in the way.

"To plan for evacuation and for an efficient emergency response following a massive flood, you need a relief map that shows the land's elevations," she said. "The relief map they have given me to use was drawn 45 years ago. It shows elevations in five-foot increments. As such, it is useless. I have been asking for a new map showing today's development—the new cities and towns and communities out west. I have asked for a map like this, with one-foot elevations, for the past two years. I'm still waiting."

APPENDIX: RECOMMENDATIONS

1. **The health care community should develop a warning system that augments the National Weather Service's standard "WATCH, WARNING" notification system. The national standard allows, at most, 48 hours warning of an impending storm. A schedule designed for the health community should allow for notification of "substantial risk" in enough time for the evacuation of special-needs, elderly, and at-risk patients from the areas most likely to be in the path of the storm.**

   Emergency agencies, relief agencies, and health care agencies in South Florida, like those in most other hurricane-prone areas, do not begin formal preparations for a severe storm until they are notified that a hurricane *watch* has been posted. The hurricane watch is usually announced 48 hours before the storm's actual landfall. At this point most hospitals begin to initiate their hurricane plans. Most other medical facilities go on alert and locate their key staff members. All of them begin to make contact with the emergency management offices in their area.

   Little else that involves extra staffing and additional expenditure is done until a hurricane *warning* is issued. Most of the time the warning is sounded about 24 hours before the first effects of the storm are expected to arrive. Because of liability issues, the EOCs do not order a mandatory evacuation of flood-prone areas or the gathering of special-needs individuals until the hurricane warning flags fly.

   Because hospitals and the rest of the health care delivery system wait until an official hurricane watch is issued before they institute emergency plans and because they wait until a hurricane warning to act, they can have no more than 24 hours to execute those plans. They wait this long for reasons having to do with logistics and justifying the cost of transporting patients, closing the facility, canceling procedures, and installing shutters. They want the crisis to be real before they act. But their desire to act only in response to a crisis becomes a self-fulfilling prophecy. Waiting until the last minute means that everything must be done at once and the potential for catastrophe increases exponentially.

If the National Weather Service provided EOCs and/or hospitals and nursing homes with warning information in percentages, then the organizations, corporations, and political subdivisions could set a timetable of activity that begins when the risk hits a predetermined percentage. Facilities could begin various preparations, including evacuation of at-risk patients, when the risk of danger exceeds 50 percent, for example, although the hurricane watch might not be posted for two more days or until the risk reaches 70 percent.

2. Hospitals and nursing homes should establish relationships among providers and facilities that are hundreds of miles apart, making these relationships contractual, if possible. Also, if possible, designate and exchange emergency teams of personnel to take part in practice drills.

Power companies and some units of the fire departments have established relationships with their counterparts at substantial distances so that they can receive backup labor and material immediately after a storm if the devastation is widespread. Hospitals rely on the next hospital, figuratively just down the street, as if a powerful storm would spare one and take the other. Their plans are based on the false supposition that the hospital will survive without being victimized and will only have to cope with casualties from beyond the hospital community. The plans anticipate an extraordinary patient load and some logistical inconvenience for a few days after the storm. They do not contemplate a total lack of power, water, and staff reinforcements. Hospitals have not planned to be victims of a storm, only to care for the victims.

Emergency medical technicians, the power companies, and fire departments are paramilitary in their organization. Their protocols and chains of command are relatively uniform and consistent wherever they operate. Medical professionals are, almost by definition, resistant to uniformity, long-term planning, and the surrender of key decisions to a central authority. Nevertheless, each hospital that is not part of a system that extends across several counties should be making arrangements with similar hospitals to swap trained staff who can become familiar with the plant during the down periods, then come in to relieve the corresponding hospital staff immediately after a storm. The primary public hospitals should be compelled to plan for the exchange of staffs in preparation for the next storm cycle.

In this remarkable era of mergers and collaborations, systems such as Columbia/Health Care America can and should play a major role in disaster preparation and organization. Columbia has the resources to support a half dozen disaster teams among its member hospitals. It has such a far-flung network of acute care and psychiatric facilities that it should be factored into the evacuation plans of hospitals even beyond its membership. There is no excuse for the for-profit hospital system, with its centralized administration, to postpone developing an exchange program among hospitals in hurricane-prone areas.

3. Modify plans so that volunteers are diverted to staging areas far away from a storm area. Assign volunteers task numbers and do not let them into the disaster area without a task number.

The story about the Winnebago full of Korean War veteran physicians heading for South Dade hell-bent for glory is both true and instructional (see Chapter 9). Immediately after a storm the needs of the affected community may be great, but they are also specific. The one thing that is needed above all else is order. What is not needed are extra people to feed, house, direct, protect, and indemnify. This is one of those rare cases when it is better to need help and not have it than to have help and not need it.

Any profession that requires licensing can incorporate into its code of conduct a standard that requires that members not be permitted to enter an emergency area to practice their licensed skill unless they are first accredited by the agency in charge of accreditation in that area. On the other side, EOCs should set up a remote accreditation center far beyond the threshold of the affected area. Professionals should be admitted as volunteers only after they are accredited and receive a task number that tells everyone where they are to work, for whom, and when.

4. Plan to be completely self-sufficient and without any food, water, power, or human backup for at least 48 hours.

This recommendation is self-evident. Even the latest revisions in the FEMA regulations allow for 24 hours before professional federal relief agents arrive, after the locals declare a need for assistance. As the Hurricane Andrew experience demonstrates, it is difficult to imagine a serious emergency in which it doesn't take the locals 24 hours to complete their assessment and begin to take remedial action. Where there is widespread damage, the 24 hours during which the damage assessment is conducted is typically followed by 24 more hours during which the human resources and equipment are marshaled that will be needed to remedy the loss of basic services and to provide emergency power and supplies.

5. **Consider modifications in the hospital and health care facilities' accreditation and licensing standards that include close scrutiny of evacuation plans and transportation arrangements for facilities that are built in evacuation areas.**

It is not sufficient for hospitals, nursing homes, and congregate living facilities built in flood-prone evacuation areas to pass health and safety inspections of their physical plants. Licensing agencies and accreditation boards must look at facilities in the context of their location and the amount of effort that will be required to evacuate them when the time comes. They must make sure that the operators have secured contractual arrangements with shelters at appropriate distances and with transportation providers who will guarantee priority service.

Of course, evacuation will more likely be successful if medical facilities begin their emergency evacuations sooner than the rest of the population.

6. **Require the hardening of all facilities not in evacuation areas.**

It is easier in theory to harden facilities than to evacuate the people the facilities are designed to serve each time a natural disaster threatens. In fact, instead of school buildings becoming default shelters, health care facilities could be built or modified to perform these functions, solving two problems at once. Tax incentives or some other compensation for the hardening of facilities would be appropriate.

7. **Restrict the addition of new health care beds in any facility in an evacuation area unless the facility can prove it has the resources to evacuate all of its potential patients.**

This is a difficult recommendation to implement. All of the populated areas of Monroe County, Florida, are in mandatory evacuation zones, for example. This would mean that hospital and nursing home construction would be curtailed in Monroe unless extraordinary evacuation plans were documented. Local decision makers should decide if this is as it should be.

8. Develop a mental health component that begins with search and rescue after the storm and that follows through for at least a year beyond the date of the storm. Make it neighbor-hood-based and integrated with the delivery of public assistance and emergency relief.

The stress of enduring the force of a major storm is sufficient to trigger mental health problems in much of the population where latent problems already exist. Statistics show that violence, substance abuse, psychosis, and suicide increase dramatically in storm-affected populations. The experience of Hurricane Andrew also showed that those who endured the storm well were often brought to the brink of mental health crises by the continuing sequence of frustrations attendant to seeking food, shelter, insurance settlements, contractors, and a decent place to stay in the meantime.

In South Florida a mental health specialist joined social service workers who called on storm victims, and expedited social services were included as a component of mental health, much to the satisfaction of everyone involved. The State of Florida ended the process prematurely, however, and made little effort for follow through, plunging victims whose expectations had been raised back into the morass of despair. Social services and mental health should be looked on as an interconnected system, community-based and ongoing long after the storm episode is past.

9. Recognize that transportation is an essential component of the public health and mental health delivery systems after the storm.

It makes no difference how quickly storm aid arrives if a system is not in place assuring access to the centralized locations where it is provided. This is especially true for indigent populations. A system of jitneys operated by drivers of various ethnic backgrounds worked extremely well in South Dade. The jitneys ran with no cost to the riders on a fairly regular schedule. They went where the people needed to go; and, almost as important, the drivers became messengers for the overall system, informing people of changes in locations and operations of facilities, spreading the word as things got worse or better. This was done ad hoc after Hurricane Andrew. Jamaicans, Haitians, and Hispanics—some licensed and others unlicensed—dominated the jitney business in South Florida. They had no formal training as facilitators and no formal system was established for them to notify public health officials about what they were seeing and hearing as they traveled beyond the front lines of the relief effort. An effort to provide these people with baseline skills and a system that would enable communication with public health authorities is worth considering.

10. **Create four sets of standardized documents for use during an emergency situation: one that can be used at every venue to track the care provided to each individual entering the emergency health care network, one that can be used for procurement in the rescue phase, one that can be used to request FEMA funds, and one that can be used for reimbursement of out-of-pocket expenses at any time during the process.**

Four sets may be more than is necessary, but there does need to be a standardization of the paper work that recognizes that storm victims who really need help probably don't have much of the usual documentation available, nor will they be able to get it. Likewise, agencies that are affected by increased demand as a result of a storm are likely to have less time to prepare requests and grant applications than they might otherwise.

11. **Advances in radio-telephonics have opened a new set of wavelengths. While this system is in the development phase and before all frequencies are assigned, set up one standard frequency or set of frequencies for all emergency communications, nationwide.**

The most glaring deficiency in the South Florida experience after Hurricane Andrew was in communication. Southern Bell's wire system collapsed, leading to an overcrowding of the wireless telephone system. Each emergency organization operated on a different wavelength, both figuratively and literally. Citizens band transmissions were impossible because of the traffic jam. Only shortwave communications worked well. But shortwave operators are set up to speak over long distances, not within a small geographic region. And they, too, need a power supply.

But emerging technology has made it possible to tune radio telephonic equipment with greater precision. And with an infinite number of points on a line, it is possible that several of those points could be set aside solely for emergency communications. Then every organization needing to send or receive information could purchase communications gear attuned to the designated frequencies. Some could be set aside for broadcast only, others for two-way communications. Call it the "information sidewalk."